AF279234

For Suz, Daniele, and Drew

Goff Books
Novato, California
Published by Goff Books, an Imprint of ORO Editions
Gordon Goff: Publisher

www.goffbooks.com
info@goffbooks.com

Author: Craig Frazier
Illustrations by Craig Frazier
Photographs by Smeeta Mahanti
Foreword by Hank Richardson
Book design by Craig Frazier
Managing Editor: Jake Anderson

10 9 8 7 6 5 4 3 2 1 First Edition

ISBN: 978-1-957183-91-6

Color Separations and Printing: ORO Group Inc.
Printed in China.

Goff Books makes a continuous effort to minimize the overall carbon footprint of its publications. As part of this goal, Goff Books, in association with Global ReLeaf, arranges to plant trees to replace those used in the manufacturing of the paper produced for its books. Global ReLeaf is an international campaign run by American Forests, one of the world's oldest nonprofit conservation organizations. Global ReLeaf is American Forests' education and action program that helps individuals, organizations, agencies, and corporations improve the local and global environment by planting and caring for trees.

Craig Frazier Drawn

goff

Contents

Foreword by Hank Richardson

Miami Ad School Atlanta, Director of Design

I met Craig Frazier twenty-five years ago, when I invited him to speak at my school. He has visited many times since. If you know Craig, it won't surprise you to hear how excited he is to interact with students—and how wide he opens their eyes. Fascinating, imaginative, and so very human, he always circles back to one simple theme: *Before you can design, you have to draw out your ideas.*

Drawn is testament to a career practicing exactly that.

There is both a timeliness and a timelessness in Craig's illustrations. He meets a client's challenge of the moment, but does it in such a way that you want to frame it for your wall, to keep forever. He has a way of stretching ideas, breaking them, and then reassembling them into inexplicably new ideas. Yet he never dilutes the gravity of the message.

In his essays, Craig demonstrates a deep devotion to his craft, as well as the giants who influenced him. He speaks with kindness, humility, honesty, and, always on cue, that well-calibrated wit. It's as if he has written the "true confessions" of a true artist, opening up about his life, learnings, and methods. How interesting it is to learn how he processes our world through his imagination, letting his ideas ooze out in illustration.

In a sense, illustration has been Craig's therapist. It created the peace he needed to look inward, to draw stories built upon human truths. It freed him to filter ideas through his personal values and charmingly odd creative sensibilities. It gave him the confidence to play unrestrained —and to invite us to play along.

You can enjoy these pages as a tourist, simply enjoying the sights, and it would be time well spent. Or you can absorb Craig's observations and inspirations to re-calibrate the way you think and create. To see the world through different eyes. Do not be daunted that Craig's work ethic is simultaneously simple and impossible: *Never have just one idea, and never stop looking.* It's an inspiring way to get where you're going.

My unfair advantage in life is that I have had the privilege of picking Craig's brain. I learned what motivates him, and how he sketches his way to such consistently amazing work. Drawn will give you the same advantage I got from twenty-five years of friendship—happily, in considerably less time.

Design Conversation:
Craig Frazier

Thursday, July 18, 2019
7:00 PM—8:30 PM
Hill Auditorium
1280 Peachtree St. NE
Atlanta, GA

Join MODA and Miami Ad School at Portfolio Center for a Design Conversation with designer & illustrator Craig Frazier

MIAMI AD SCHOOL
@PORTFOLIO CENTER

MODA

Introduction by Craig Frazier

Born to draw.

 "Look at what I did!" I said that frequently as a kid seeking an audience for my drawings. I still do.

The drawing we do in our early years may be the most honest and unfettered drawing we'll ever do, because we draw without judgment. Only later in life do we get judged for the first time by someone else, or worse—by ourselves. It's when we realize we can't quite make things look how they appear that many of us quit drawing. I remember that feeling, but I didn't quit. I was having too much fun.

And the fun would continue. It was *Mad* magazine that opened my eyes to commercial drawing. The magazine was chock-full of cartoons and caricatures by famous illustrators, each of whom drew in a distinct style. Wit, humor, and general irreverence were the mainstay of *Mad* illustrations. For me, that magazine became a source of drawing lessons, and exposure to styles of illustration that were impossible to get in school.

Only rock 'n' roll.

By high school, the rock posters of the '60s and '70s replaced *Mad's* snarky influence in my life. There were the posters of Peter Max, so wondrous in their expression—colorful, whimsical, and drawn with his signature calligraphic line. Ironically, there was Seymour Chwast's anti-Vietnam "End Bad Breath" poster, which I hung in my bedroom in my military home. Next came the influence of rock album cover art, which was a treasure trove of some of the best illustration of the time. I recall Rod Stewart's *Atlantic Crossing* painted in airbrush by Peter Lloyd. And Tom Wilkes's sublime lettering on Neil Young's *Harvest*—an epic signature to the songwriting within. There was Emerson, Lake & Palmer's *Brain Salad Surgery*, drawn by H. R. Giger, and the surreal Yes covers by Roger Dean, to name but a few. By high school's end, I began to make the connection between drawing and popular culture. I would spend the next four years in college learning the requisite skills to make my entry into that world—better known as graphic design.

Elementary School drawing, 1963

A designed career.

I have been fortunate to make my livelihood employing my love for drawing. My career has taken many turns, demanding that I learn new skills and practices in order to stay in the game. But drawing has been the constant.

This book is about the ride.

My career, which began in my early twenties, continues to this day. So far, it can be divided into two parts. First, I was a graphic designer who liked to draw. Then I became an illustrator who knows how to design. This book is primarily devoted to the latter—the body of my work as an illustrator and the discipline required to create it.

It's important to note that, while my career has a dividing line, the experiences on either side define the same career. As it would turn out, being a designer was the ideal preparatory course for my career as an illustrator. My orientation toward problem-solving and the skills I learned over my twenty years as a designer would become the foundation of my practice as an illustrator. They formed the particular lens through which I approach every drawing today.

My path to becoming an illustrator was not exactly typical, and I suppose this is reflected in the work itself. According to several of my peers, it's evident that my inner designer still breathes. While I'm flattered by this observation, I consider illustration to be the deeper development of my creative life. My work as an illustrator has exposed me to far more clients, businesses, and subjects—all around the world—than my younger self ever imagined possible. This book satisfies my urge to look for the connective tissue in the work I've done over the decades. The designer in me says I would be foolish not to organize such an inquiry into the pages of a book.

Dissecting the muse.

In these pages, I group drawings by their content. As an example, I might pair a drawing made in the year 2000 with a re-visitation of a similar theme or metaphor fifteen years later. The first section is devoted to the earliest days of my work as an official illustrator and the last features my most current work at the time of this book's publishing. I now see the naivete in many of those early drawings, yet their principles remain present in the work decades later.

I have devoted a section titled "By hand" to my process. It's my own fascination with others' processes that inspires me to share mine. In my experience, a glimpse at the otherwise unseen underpinnings of one's practice tends to reveal new meaning in a person's finished product and, more important, an understanding of the work required to get there. The irony of illustration is that behind every illustrator's body of finished work lies a mountain of sketches, false starts, and rejected ideas—often as good as or even better than our publicly seen work. Along with sketches and sketchbooks, I'm including a sampling of my cut Amberliths, which I make for every illustration. Though I complete my work digitally, I remain of the mind that the longer I can keep my hand in the process, the more humanity I can instill in the drawing.

Most of the drawings within this book are for clients—individuals, companies, and publications all over the world. My common objective has been to help those clients speak visually with distinction, optimism, and illumination to their varied audiences. Though perhaps artistic, this work is not art; it is creating drawings designed to do a job. It is creativity in the service of business—a mutually beneficial relationship.

Drawing for meaning.

For me, it is essential that my illustrations be injected with humor, wit, and surprise. Yet that's the tricky part, because it requires clients to believe that information and entertainment aren't mutually exclusive. While I am hired to build clients' brands, doing so depends on how well they believe in my brand of thinking—and drawing. My best work has been made for those believers. Thank you all.

To curate the drawings contained in this book, I had to measure the work against personal criteria. A work's commercial success—or lack thereof—has no bearing on its inclusion. I have presented what I consider is my best, or at least my most interesting, work. Each piece had to satisfy three other requirements: be provocative in and of itself, without any explanatory text; be beautiful; and lastly, bring a smile to your mind.

Building character.

Design and illustration can be all-consuming careers, especially if you want to survive for very long. I'll admit, taking on both can be doubly consuming. However, without immersion it's unlikely that certain roads would be taken nor lessons be learned. Ultimately, the conditions under which we work shape the character of that work—a sort of call and response. I've tried to recount some of the more interesting stories.

This is for you.

I've designed this book to speak to as many people as possible. First, I feel a certain responsibility to present my experience to the designers, illustrators, photographers, artists, and writers who have shared the road with me. You have inspired and challenged me, and I hope you will see a bit of yourselves within these pages. Second, I want to share my understanding of making work in a tough business to the students and young practitioners making their way. The profession is ever-changing, and I'm counting on you to discover unique points of view—to make wonderfully creative contributions despite the forces that promote "sameness" as good enough. Your voice counts and will ultimately propel you into the conversation. Third, I want to speak to the clients and consumers of creativity in business. I hope to lift the hood on the instincts that work within all creative beings, and show that—if left unbridled, supported, and rewarded fairly—those instincts will pay back in immeasurable imagination, content, and good will.

Last, I want to speak to anyone, at any stage in life, who desires to give agency to their life's experience and views. I have learned that purpose must be the central pursuit of our work, and everything else follows. I want to speak to those facing hard choices involving work, money, family, and the itch to find a rewarding connection between who we are and what we do. The return on taking risks and feeding curiosity comes in the form of friendships, invention, and the deep satisfaction of being in the arena.

At least, that's been my experience.

Prologue

Drawing lessons.

When I was in third grade, my teacher noticed that I liked to draw, perhaps more than the other students. So, I was assigned to draw a Mercator projection of the earth on a twelve-foot piece of white paper to cover the entire expanse of the bulletin board at the front of the classroom. At that moment, I learned that I had a talent that could lead to special treatment. While the rest of the class was working on arithmetic, I was breathing Magic Marker fumes free-handing Africa. Intoxicating as it was, this didn't translate into an interest in geography—but it did leave an impression on me that I should probably keep drawing.

Three years later, I took a summer class in which I did my first pen-and-ink drawing. It felt different than drawing with other tools, which were usually pencils, crayons, or felt pens. They had a certain "art" quality to them. The class had a competition and I won first prize. (I think there were only three other kids in the class.) I'm not sure what I liked better, the drawing or the blue ribbon!

All through elementary school, I felt the urge to draw anything and everything. I practiced, but what I wanted most were school projects where I could work on a sheet of poster board with those fragrant markers. I was usually drawing diagrams or objects, quite often combined with hand lettering to illustrate a fact or tell a story. I had no idea that those were the fundamentals of graphic design.

Unsettled.

I didn't have an ordinary childhood. My dad was an Air Force officer, which dictated that we move from one air base to another every two years or so. That gave me a taste of New Mexico, Texas, and California. Air Force brats don't typically develop lifelong childhood friends because one or the other tends to move before deep friendships are cemented. No doubt this informed a particular introduction to solitude and time alone—all requisites to being an illustrator.

Then, it happened again. My interest in drawing bought me a pass. I was in eighth grade and my dad was receiving an award at the Pentagon. He was an engineer and designed something that saved the government a lot of money—an act that didn't go unnoticed. Our family was invited to Washington, DC, for a week of celebration in the middle of the school year. This was a "no-miss" event for me, so my art teacher negotiated with my other teachers to let me make sketches of the trip. My sketches would be presented—along with a report—to each class in exchange for class time missed. The pattern of drawing in barter for curriculum continued.

On that trip I visited the Lincoln Memorial, the Capitol, The Tomb of the Unknown Soldier, the Arlington Memorial, and the Washington Monument. My parents would drop me off and return an hour later to pick me up after I'd made a pen-and-ink

New Mexico, 1965

drawing of each of them. It was 1968, a time when a teenager could safely walk around in Washington unchaperoned. This exercise turned out to be my first journalism assignment, though at the time I had no idea this was an actual profession. A week later, I presented the drawings to my classes, fulfilling my end of the bargain—perhaps planting the tiniest seed that drawing might become a valuable talent.

Regrettably, those drawings were lost in the disarray of my parents' divorce two years later, never holding the significance to them that they did to me.

Post-divorce, in my junior year in high school, I returned to California from New Mexico with my brother and my mom, finally free of the military. I felt unusually grown up and lost at the same time. I continued my drawing, though not seriously enough to be more than a hobby. At the same time, I was taking architectural drawing classes learning perfunctory drafting skills. While my work was frequently singled out as a demonstration of how to scribe a perfect graphite line, I was intrigued and somewhat tempted by the field of architecture. The praise might have clouded my judgment, but the truth is that I loved making the line—whatever the subject.

Self-portrait, graphite, Chico, California, 1978

Like most teenagers, I didn't feel particularly comfortable with my talents. Perhaps that was appropriate, as I was untrained and at an early stage of artistic development. Nevertheless, I would retreat to drawing with greater frequency. By my senior year in high school, I knew I was supposed to be thinking about what I might want to do for a living, or at least what I should choose as a major in college. Neither were apparent to me. Coincidentally, my mom remarried, this time to a psychologist, which seemed to spark an interest in that field. However, I kept wondering if there might be an option that involved drawing.

Intro to graphic design.
Just prior to taking off for college, my mom introduced me to a friend who was a graphic designer. A profession I had never heard of. I visited the studio where the man designed greeting cards and ephemera—all nice, but nothing particularly distinct. What did leave an impression upon me was that he made a living drawing. This may have been the best parental introduction of my life.

So, I started college and dutifully enrolled in "Intro to Psychology." At the same time, I signed up for "Intro to Graphic Design," which was a required class for lithography majors. The school didn't offer a formal graphic design degree at that time.

The graphic design class opened up a whole new world to me from the first day. The most memorable lesson was that every company's logo I saw was drawn by someone. Aha, there are actual jobs that require drawing! The following semester, I dropped my psychology classes and took all the available design classes with additional electives in life drawing and printmaking. I also took illustration as an extracurricular class, only to learn that there was an adjunct career to graphic design—freelance illustrator.

A society of illustrators.
In my senior year, I had an internship at the campus graphics department and found myself drawing spot illustrations for brochures and posters. Technically, I was most comfortable drawing in line and cross-hatch but experimented with more graphic expressions, perhaps influenced by my logo classes. The hidden benefit of this internship was access to

Life drawing, *pen and ink*
Chico State University, 1977

College internship illustration
Moscow Travel pamphlet
Pen and ink,1978

College internship poster
Ink, 2-color offset, 1978

College block print
Ink on paper, 1978

the college's library of Society of Illustrators annuals, which featured the country's greatest illustrators and showcased the myriad styles of each year. I took one book home every night and pored over the contents, absorbing the work of the superstars of illustration —Bernie Fuchs, Mark English, Milton Glaser, Bob Peak, Robert Heindel, Murray Tinkleman, Rafael Oblinski, Doug Johnson, Jean Michel Folon, Guy Billout, and Michael David Brown, to name but a few who resonated with me personally. The takeaway from my nightly study into the work of these giants was that every illustrator had his or her own distinct style, which was their professional identity—their calling card. I was smitten.

The illustrations of that time were predominantly paintings which, as much as I loved, I could not see myself doing. I was petrified by painting and color, and lacked the schooling. However, there was the conceptual pen-and-ink work of those like Alan Cober, Brad Holland, and Jack Unruh, that spoke to me in ways I couldn't fully comprehend at the time. And then there were illustrators like Patrick Nagel, Seymour Chwast, and Don Weller, whose work was flat, graphic and stylized—which I was drawn to perhaps due to their simplification of form and idea.

By graduation, I had freelance illustrated for a local design firm and built a design portfolio with an emphasis on drawing. I also met renowned Berkeley poster designer David Lance Goines, whose graphic style of melding image and concept cast illustration in a brand-new light to me. He was not only a designer and illustrator, he was a printer. Clients waited in line for more than a year to have their posters designed by him. Along with his masterful style, David left the clear impression that our work could—and probably should—be personal. That lesson was etched in my mind. At this point, I was slowly connecting the dots between drawing and design. I would graduate college with a major in graphic design and move one hundred miles south to pursue a life in design in the San Francisco Bay Area, where I was hired to be a budding designer. I later learned I got the job because I could draw. Things only got better from there.

Note: The last annual I borrowed from that library was *Illustrators 19*. It would be twenty-three years later that my work would appear on the cover of *The Society of Illustrators 42*.

Illustrators 19
Society of Illustrators
Annual, 1978

Freelance illustration
Chico Chamber of
Commerce brochure
Ink, 4-color offset, 1978

By Hand poster
David Lance Goines, 1974

Illustrators 42
Society of Illustrators
Annual, 2000

San Francisco design.

In the late '70s and early '80s, the San Francisco Bay Area was gaining a reputation as a design community independent of its neighbor 500 miles south (Los Angeles). Those in architecture, cultural arts, music, furniture, financial services, paper companies, publishing, real estate development, and technology were eager to give graphic design a key role in their business. Though there were a few large corporate identity firms and ad agencies, it was a handful of young design firms that were creating work that would become identified as "San Francisco design." A small but tight community was beginning to flourish, as competitive as it was collegial. It was a brand of design that was easily recognized, with graphics that were bold, simple, colorful, and elegant—a certain recalibration of Swiss graphic design of the '50s. It presented an optimism and playfulness that reflected the sun-drenched, carefree spirit of the city with a dash of '60s rock 'n' roll posters.

1978 was a perfect time to start a design career. My first job out of college was at a new design firm in Palo Alto, California, about thirty-five miles south of San Francisco. The region was becoming known by the nickname "Silicon Valley"—a name that accurately predicted the future. Several of our clients were early tech companies that manufactured chips and components for mainframe computers. Personal computers were still in their infancy, and Apple was a long way from becoming ubiquitous among design firms. I didn't fully realize I was working at the center of an industry that would change the entire design business and our culture at the same time.

I left Palo Alto in 1980 to open a studio in San Francisco with a partner, Conrad Jorgensen. Non-tech opportunities appeared plentiful. We rented a cramped office in a landmark building on Union Square with two drawing tables, a conference table made of a door and two sawhorses, and a rented IBM Selectric typewriter. I got married within six months of opening our doors. Life was so exciting, we forgot to be scared.

To the dismay of my former employers, one of their better clients left with me—the reward for being the principal designer on the business. They were a rising management consulting firm headquartered on Palo Alto's legendary Sand Hill Road. This association got us out of the starting block and would keep us

Trademark, Spectum Marketing
Pacific Telephone, 1983

Trademark
Photo stylist, 1985

Brand hangtag
Levi's Strauss, 1984

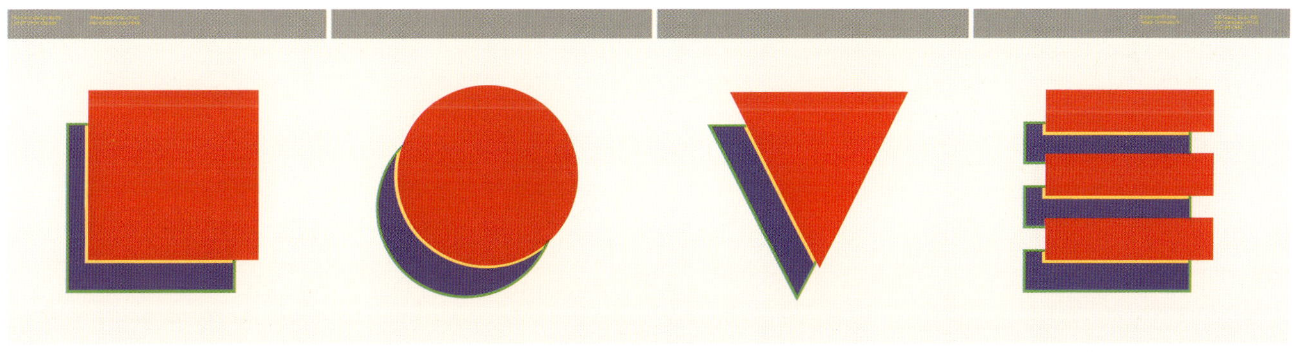

Human Relations Services icons
McKesson Corporation, 1983

Poster announcing of our new studio
Five-color silkscreen, 9" x 28" unfolded
Jorgensen/Frazier Design, 1980

Season poster
San Francisco Ballet, 1979

Event poster
AIGA/ San Francisco, 1989

Event poster
AIGA/ San Francisco, 1989

going for years to come. Of course, our fledgling firm took on any work that came our way—in health care and communications (Pacific Telephone), and with paper companies, record companies, printers, apparel companies, and ad agencies.

Despite growing to function like a real design firm, the partnership unraveled after a few years of success. We would learn how different our work styles actually were. The truth is that without each other and our collective ambition, we would never have braved opening a design firm with such little experience amidst a city with such talented competition. It served to be a great proving ground to launch us both onto our own future paths.

My firm would become Craig Frazier Design, which grew into an office capable of managing numerous and varied projects. By this time, Silicon Valley was bursting with high-tech companies, with new ones springing up every day. The internet was still off in the future, but there was seemingly endless work in the world of personal and enterprise computing. The video game market was white hot. Print design was at an all-time high point as companies were producing lavish annual reports, human resources packages, software packaging, catalogs, posters, brochures, and data sheets aplenty. If you were asked to design the new company logo, it could well lead to more projects as the company grew. While there was an abundance of work to be won, there was a corresponding surge of new design firms trying to win it. Building a reputation meant always looking over our shoulder. It became clear that steady hustling was a given, but what mattered most was doing distinct, recognizable work. The answer was to make my work more illustrative.

Designers like Nicolas Sidjakov, John Casado, Michael Vanderbyl, Michael Manwaring, Michael Cronan, Kit Hinrichs, Michael Mabry, Michael Schwab, and I shared the ability to draw pretty well, which was evident in our work. We were collectively creating a design aesthetic that was undeniably colorful, simple, graphic—often whimsical. Though it would often appear that some designers were going through other's trash, there were stylistic distinctions evident to the trained eye. Nevertheless, there were times when all of the work looked like it had the same parents. I was very aware that "sameness" was ultimately the enemy, and if I was to survive, I had to keep working at being different.

Over the next decade, I found my own voice—but not without a nod to my San Francisco roots.

Employee event poster
Pacific Telephone, 1981

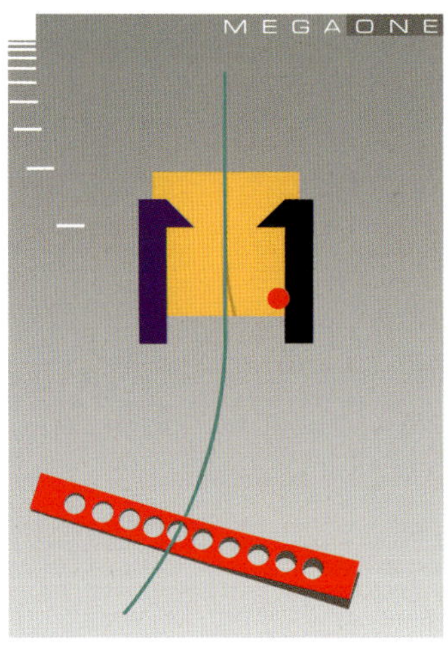

MegaOne technology poster
Megatest, 1988

Summer Season poster
San Francisco Opera, 1986

SIMPSON STOCKMAN

Corporate services poster
Simpson Paper Company, 1981

The common thread.

For me, solving any design problem begins with drawing—and in many cases ends with drawing. It has been the through line in my career.

I graduated college with the fantasy that I could become an illustrator. With the advice of several designers, I realized that I was unprepared to be an illustrator, and design better suited my skills. I was, however, hired for my first job because I could draw. In 1980, the business required it. Designers had to draw prototypes to communicate our intentions to clients. Any visual—photograph, illustration, and often typography—was shown as a sketch first to get client approval. Drawing was the essential first step in any design, and happily I was qualified.

But I was interested in more than just drawing prototype designs for client approval. I was interested in drawing the actual design that would become ink on paper. From the start, I was drawn to, and influenced by, designers who could draw—particularly in very graphic styles. The works of designers like Paul Rand, Ivan Chermayeff, Don Weller, Saul Bass, Milton Glaser, and Takenobu Igarashi were easily identified by their unique illustrations within. There was something that set their work apart from so much of the design of that time. It presented a certain humanity and accessibility that only comes from the hand of a designer who draws.

In my last year in college, I met Berkeley poster designer David Lance Goines, and was taken by the ideas and execution within every one of his posters. After a workshop with him, I learned how personal his work was to his values and his life—that one's

work should reflect their innate sensibilities. I learned that beauty could be more than decoration, and could in fact be the vehicle to express ideas. The designer's brain is inextricably connected to his hand.

Perhaps the most significant contribution of drawing to my design was that I kept a sketchbook, and always started a project with thumbnails and notes. This is a discipline that I've applied to every project I have ever done—start small and simple, and avoid rushing toward execution. I've maintained the discipline of ideation and "walking around" a problem looking for a way in, always guided by a pen line. The immediacy of sketching small and quickly on paper forces the mind to see possibilities as new images emerge. It is a kind of visual "telephone game" where a simple sketch sets off a reaction in another sketch and then another—often with inexplicable connection. It's a muse that reveals ideas like magic.

For the next sixteen years as a designer (1980–1996), I gravitated toward designing solutions that were innately graphic, which I frequently drew myself. Whether it was a chart for an annual report, a logo for a sporting event, or a poster—I always tried to bring personality and character by drawing it by hand. For example, the logo for LucasArts may have been one of the most unusual logos I've designed. It was an anti-logo by its nature—unpolished and rough and strange and friendly. Rather than use technical drawing pens to produce perfect forms, I drew this figure with a spackling knife resulting in an almost petroglyphic character (page 26). Who would have imagined it would still be a cult favorite amongst video gamers twenty years later.

Nutcracker poster
San Francisco Ballet, 1989

Nutcracker
SAN FRANCISCO BALLET
Helgi Tomasson, Artistic Director
Dec. 12-31, 1989
War Memorial
Opera House
Original choreography by Lew Christensen,
with additional choreography and staging
by Willam Christensen and Helgi Tomasson.
Scenery and Costumes by Jose Varona.
Lighting by David K. H. Elliott.
Tickets available at the San Francisco Ballet
Box Office in the Opera House, at all BASS/
Ticketmaster Centers or CALL 762-BASS NOW!

Poster/ad, *Sober graduation awareness*
Marin High Schools, California, 1993

Season ticket brochure
San Franciso Opera, 1986

DesignLines magazine
The Merchandising Mart, 1989

Editorial illustration
The Olympic Club,1994

Trademark
Interstar Releasing Films, 1994

Athletic event logo, *Ride 'n Tie*
Levi's Strauss, 1986

Film company logo
Legname/Bermann, 1992

Trademark
Wildflower Seed Company, 1986

White Tiger fundraiser identity
San Francisco Zoo, 1988

Identity & illustration
San Franciso Opera, 1986

Trademark
LucasArts, 1992

Printer promotional poster
Cut paper printed six PMS colors
James H. Barry Printers, 1988

The James H. Barry Printing Company. In style for over 105 years.

Retail posters (silkscreen)
Macy's/Casio, 1981

Original ink drawing on
Duralene with .000 Rapidograph
Macy's/Casio, 1981

A kid could do that.

A surprise project taught me to see very differently. I was designing a small book (3.75" x 5.5") for a client and, due to print production requirements, we had room for another little book on the press sheet. An opportunity to experiment! However, I learned this only two days before going to press. In this compressed timeframe, I needed twenty-eight images that could fill a fifty-six-page booklet—a daunting number to produce in such limited time.

I looked around for a jumping-off point. Just so happened that my kids were one and four, and both were constantly drawing. That night, I pulled out a stack of their drawings, trying to understand why they were so good. What was present was an innocence and fearlessness captured with great energy and the fewest of strokes. Both had the ability to represent something with little concern for likeness of representation. The definition of finding essence in simplicity.

This was the nudge I needed to formulate an idea. It needed to be simple and quick, and at the very least, fun. The prompt I gave myself for each drawing was to use a 1.5" piece of black masking tape to create some sort of creature—real or imagined. The only rule was that I had to use every piece of the tape. The hole I made for an eye became an ear. Stripes became legs. Arms became horns. Scraps became appendages. Limitations became opportunities.

My kids' drawings became a guiding influence in my way of approaching each piece of tape. I became less intentional. I let the illustrations become a cut-and-respond sort of play. It was a far more spontaneous approach than I was used to—both reckless and intuitive. It didn't hurt that there was no client, no communications objective, and no expectation for what this would become. The deadline served to discourage overworking of the sticky creatures.

I made twenty-six "tape critters" by the deadline and they were bound in books the next week!

The project was as fun as it was rewarding. I turned the little book into a promotion piece for both my design firm and the printer. What started out as a frivolous, fun exercise rendered benefits far beyond our expectations. People loved the carefree book of creatures, which surprisingly turned into real business on numerous occasions. One of them was the design of a typeface for Adobe called Critter (following page).

I learned three lessons: 1) don't try too hard, 2) don't have unreasonably high expectations, and 3) share the fun you have with others.

In the next year, I went on to produce two more books and a total of eighty-four tape critters. People smiled, and new doors opened.

Tape Critters books (3)
Watermark Press, Craig Frazier Studio, San Francisco, 1990

  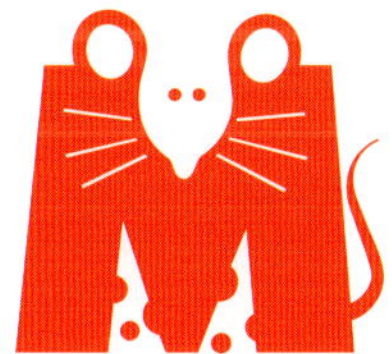 
 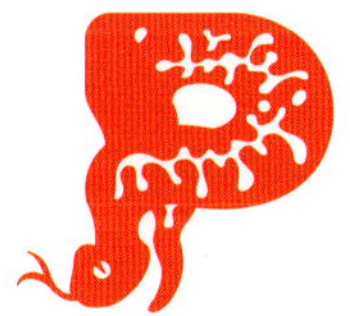  

Critter font
Adobe, 1990

The poster that changed it all.

In 1992, I was invited to design the Mill Valley Film Festival poster. I was running my six-person design firm, and this offered a welcome respite from the steady flow of technology and office furniture projects in the studio. The larger draw was that I had started the mental conversation of what it might be like to pursue a career in illustration. I had no idea that this project would answer some lingering questions and push me to the edge of that life change.

The Mill Valley Film Festival was in its fifth year and gaining the reputation as a premier US film festival, similar to its international colleagues in Cannes, Berlin, and Venice. Not sure why I got the call, but it didn't hurt that I lived in Mill Valley and I'd designed posters for the San Francisco Ballet and San Francisco Opera. I was also willing to do it for free. What the client didn't know was that I was going to try my luck at being a real illustrator.

Having previously designed a number of pro bono projects, I had some rules that I enforced. First, the project would not be a back-and-forth collaboration with the client. Second, I would endeavor to get out of my own comfort zone—try something new. My "no collaboration" rule meant I would present a near-finished design and not invite critique. This is protection against what often happens with non-profit groups. They try to help you solve the problem when you've already solved it. The Festival turned out to be a model client. They wanted something unexpected, and were willing to listen and let that process unfold.

I presented them with a finished illustration that I had hand-cut from Pantone paper. Since no single movie represented the festival, I chose the classic love story for the poster theme. I cast Adam and Eve together in the garden, looking longingly at one another. Rather than the expected fig leaves, I placed film strips over their privates. I handwrote the text. Nothing about the poster was overthought or fussy. It had a certain freshness to it. They loved it.

The graphic hand-cut rendering, the subtle wit, the color, the humor—and the fun of doing it—would turn out to be signposts for a career that lay ahead.

Poster
Mill Valley Film Festival, 1992

The Mill Valley Film Festival
Oct. 1–11, 1992 Sequoia Theatre

Field test.

In 1995, I was seriously considering shuttering my design business and taking a shot at a second career in illustration. Nervous about making this switch, I tried an experiment to see if it was a good idea. The studio had a steady flow of projects that provided opportunities to conduct a test with real clients. So I hired myself to illustrate an annual report I was designing. What I would learn was priceless.

This project was perfect for illustration. The client was The Energy Foundation, a nonprofit organization that was addressing the challenges of energy and imminent climate and culture change. The report was proposing that electric cars were the future if we were to arrest the environmental impact of burning fossil fuel. Today, for most, that is a foregone conclusion, but back then there was a case to be made. The illustrations had to make the written arguments digestible and compelling. This was a perfect test for me to learn to distill the essence of a message.

The opening illustration (right) had but one purpose—present the argument that electric cars are a critical choice in shaping the future of our planet's climate. My solution looked pretty simple, which is always the goal. Since the argument was about altering the path we are on, I needed to identify the problem to be solved. Simple. Tailpipe carbon emissions equal doom. Doom to the environment and its inhabitants. The main goal of the illustration was to show that the problem is binary, with only one intelligent choice. Sometimes the message has to be emphatic to be clear.

The report was a success, and we helped move the needle. As for me, I felt a participation and contribution that I never felt just designing. I could get used to this.

For a two-year period, I would continue to test my ability to wear the hat of a designer and the new hat of the illustrator. I designed another annual report about cyber security (page 38), a services brochure introducing cloud computing (page 54), and a film festival poster (page 35).

I was conducting an experiment that was necessary lest I make a mistake I could not undo. I was looking to quell some fears before I took the leap. Could I make illustrations that were up to the standard of those made by my revered peers? Could I leverage my past skills as a designer? Could I learn to draw well enough? Could I get work? Could I still support my family?

Most of the questions I could answer with reasonable assurance. The last question was the big unknown. Having built a design firm that supported my family, for the first time I was risking something I couldn't afford to lose. This was a different kind of fear. With the words from my wife, "You'll be much happier, you can do this, we'll be fine," I made my decision. She was right.

Annual report
The Energy Foundation, 1995

Annual report
Symantec Corporation, 1995

Annual report
The Energy Foundation, 1995

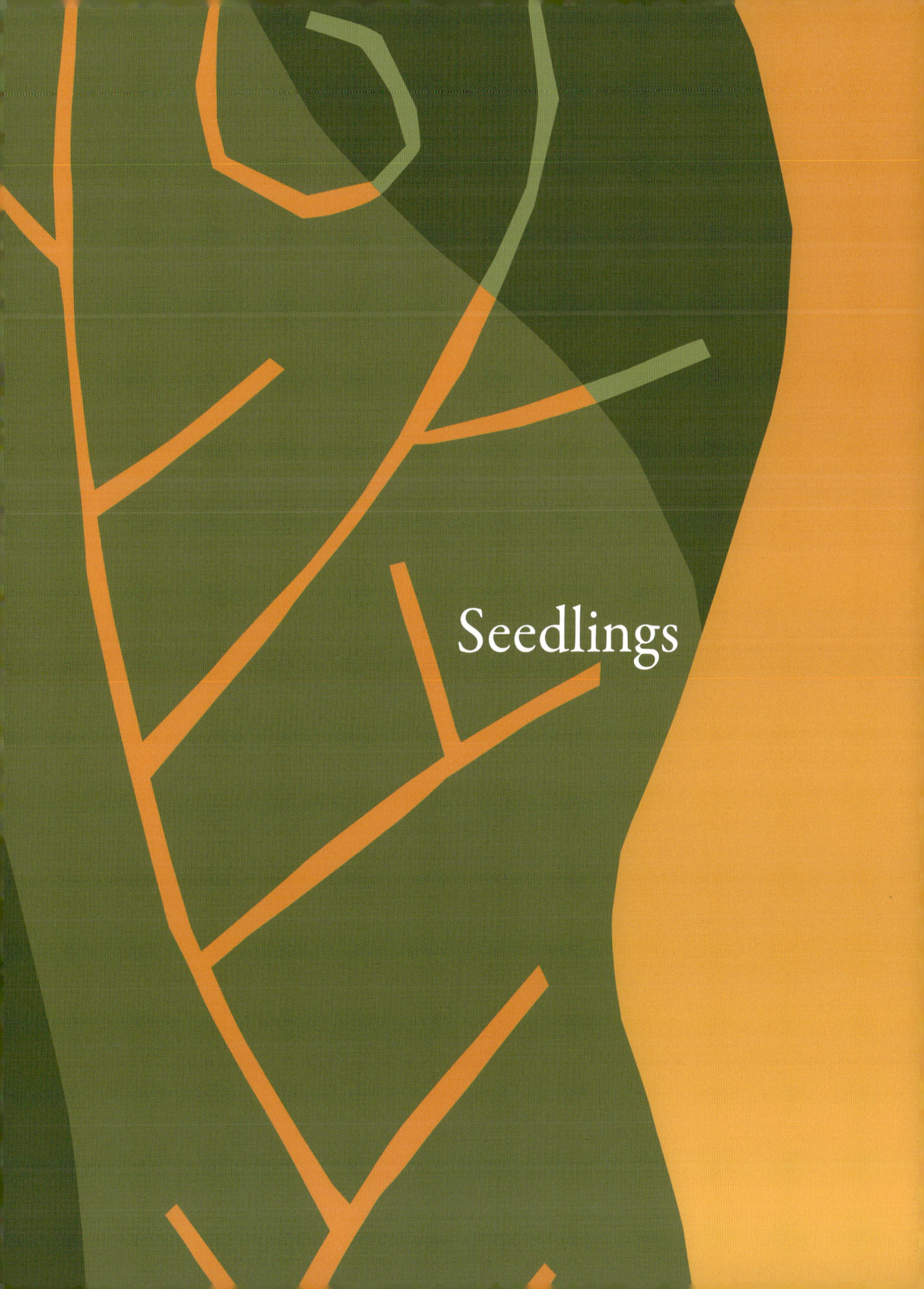

Seedlings

From here to there.

The hardest part of starting a business is getting started. Yet beginning a second career as an illustrator didn't feel that hard. The biggest reason, no doubt, was that my previous five years had laid the groundwork. I had done the homework and I wasn't afraid it wouldn't work. I just didn't know what life would be like as an illustrator, or if I would even like it. I had essentially eliminated the "first-day jitters" by putting a toe in the illustration business, while at the same time running my design business. I had already had a "soft opening."

And so I released my employees, packed up my boxes, sold my furniture, found a new office, hung up my ties and slacks, and turned out the lights on the design firm. That day, an enormous weight was lifted from my shoulders—and a new, lighter weight took its place. My feet were barely touching the ground.

The second hardest thing about starting a business is learning how to get business. Having to hustle to grow the design firm gave me a head start. After running a seven-person design firm, becoming a freelance illustrator is a move down the food chain. Myriad responsibilities and engagements simply vanished. Those who were once competitors were now potential clients. I knew a lot of the best designers across the country, and they knew me, and I wasn't afraid to ask them for work. Not only did I start getting good projects, I was buoyed by well-wishes and words of support for what appeared to others to be a brazen career move. What initially was doubt turned to reasonable assuredness.

Fewer cooks in the kitchen

A fundamental difference in design and illustration is the clientele. In general, designers work directly for companies, whereas illustrators work for designers and art directors—one step removed from the actual client. Design projects tend to be complex and involve lots of people, rounds of approvals, meetings, alterations, and protracted timetables. Illustrations tend to involve fewer people, few or no meetings, and short deadlines—fewer moving parts. At this point in my life, I was ready for the latter.

One of the great benefits of working directly with designers was that we speak with a common vocabulary. My new clientele were generally more attuned to the styles of illustrators, making it more likely that I'd be called into projects that were the right philosophical fit. My inner designer understood the context in which my illustration had to function, so I knew the right questions to ask.

I expected that all of these factors would make for a new efficiency in my job. I found myself working for people who had not only shared my goal of producing notable work—they expected it from me.

Advertising
Carter Cosgrove, 1997

Promotional brochure
Craig Frazier Studio, 1995

Style guide

I knew for certain that illustrators live and die by their style. But I also knew that style is far more than what the work looks like. It has its roots in the methods and patterns of thinking we consistently apply to our work. It is what we do that others do not—our personal point of view.

I realized that in defining style this way, I was translating my design principles directly into my illustration. I was building a belief system around how my illustrations were supposed to work and allowing that to inform what they would look like. It's working from the outside in—very much form following function. I was dedicated to creating work that was simple in appearance and complex in meaning. Illustrations that employed wit and metaphor—riddles that asked something of the viewer. I wanted

to work in symbols and codes that add up to new and smart ways of thinking about things. I wanted to employ understatement, leaving breadcrumbs so the reader could arrive at their own conclusions—a sort of programmed ambiguity. I wanted to contribute to my clients' designed pages and, more than anything, make work that was memorable. I wanted it to be beautiful. I wanted it to matter.

This approach would eventually gain me the reputation for illustrating complicated and even mundane subjects in ways that made them simple, accessible, and memorable.

The beauty of illustration as a career is that you get to practice every day. Every project is another step toward greater skill. The reality is that you cannot suddenly have a style—it arrives when it's ready.

Cover, *Most Promising Leaders*
Time Magazine, 1994

Corporate collateral
USI Consulting Group, 1998

Drawn to the light.

Perhaps the most important drawing lesson for me was learning to notice light. When you look closely at an object, it is the light's play on the surfaces that constructs our perception. The transition from light to shadow is what creates detail to our eye. The harder the light, the more defined that transitional edge is. Without light, there is no shadow. It is the relationship between the two that defines the entire equation for form and volume.

My first exposure to light was life drawing in my freshman year in college. I learned that when you draw the shadows, the light becomes evident. This was a breakthrough moment, when I began to draw what I was seeing, not how I thought the subject should appear. I would move around the model until I could see an interesting interplay of light and shadow to draw—the more dramatic, the easier to see and draw.

Fast-forward to my years of directing photography. The '80s and '90s were the age of large-format photography of still-life subjects using 8" x 10" film cameras. I was fortunate to work with some of the best in the country—Rudi Legname and Terry Heffernan to name just two—both masters of single-light photography producing distinctly graphic images. Most photographers used multiple lights and fill cards to evenly illuminate the subject. The result, in my opinion, were photographs that overtold the story and sacrificed drama for detail. It's the darkness and mystery in the shadows that draws us in. We can't help but be intrigued by what might exist in those unlit areas.

The 1990s and 2000s saw the rise of portrait photography as the corporate world humanized itself by featuring employees and telling stories about people. I worked with a number of these photographers— William Coupon for one—and again found myself drawn to the single light, a more dramatic rendering of the subject. This is also known as Chiaroscuro, where a portion of the subject is allowed to fall into near darkness. The beauty of this technique in portraits is that we can complete the person's face in our mind with only half the information. A subtle trick to invite the viewer's participation in understanding the photograph.

It was precisely this education in lighting that would inform my earliest illustrations and ventures into iconography. Reducing a subject to mere black-and-white required me to define the light source—even if imaginary. I wasn't interested in any level of rendering or shading. I wanted to make high contrast, graphic drawings. The results could be anything from solid silhouettes to dramatic rim-lit subjects. Inspired by the photography I was trained on, I found myself drawing the absence of detail to create intrigue for the viewer. This would evolve into a manifesto for my design and illustration for years to come.

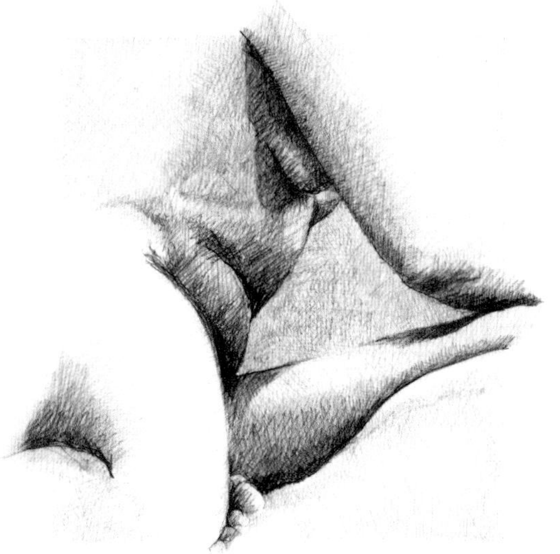

Life drawing, *graphite*
Chico State University, 1977

Sitting in for lighting test at photoshoot by
William Coupon at Steelcase Headquarters.
Grand Rapids, Michigan, 1991

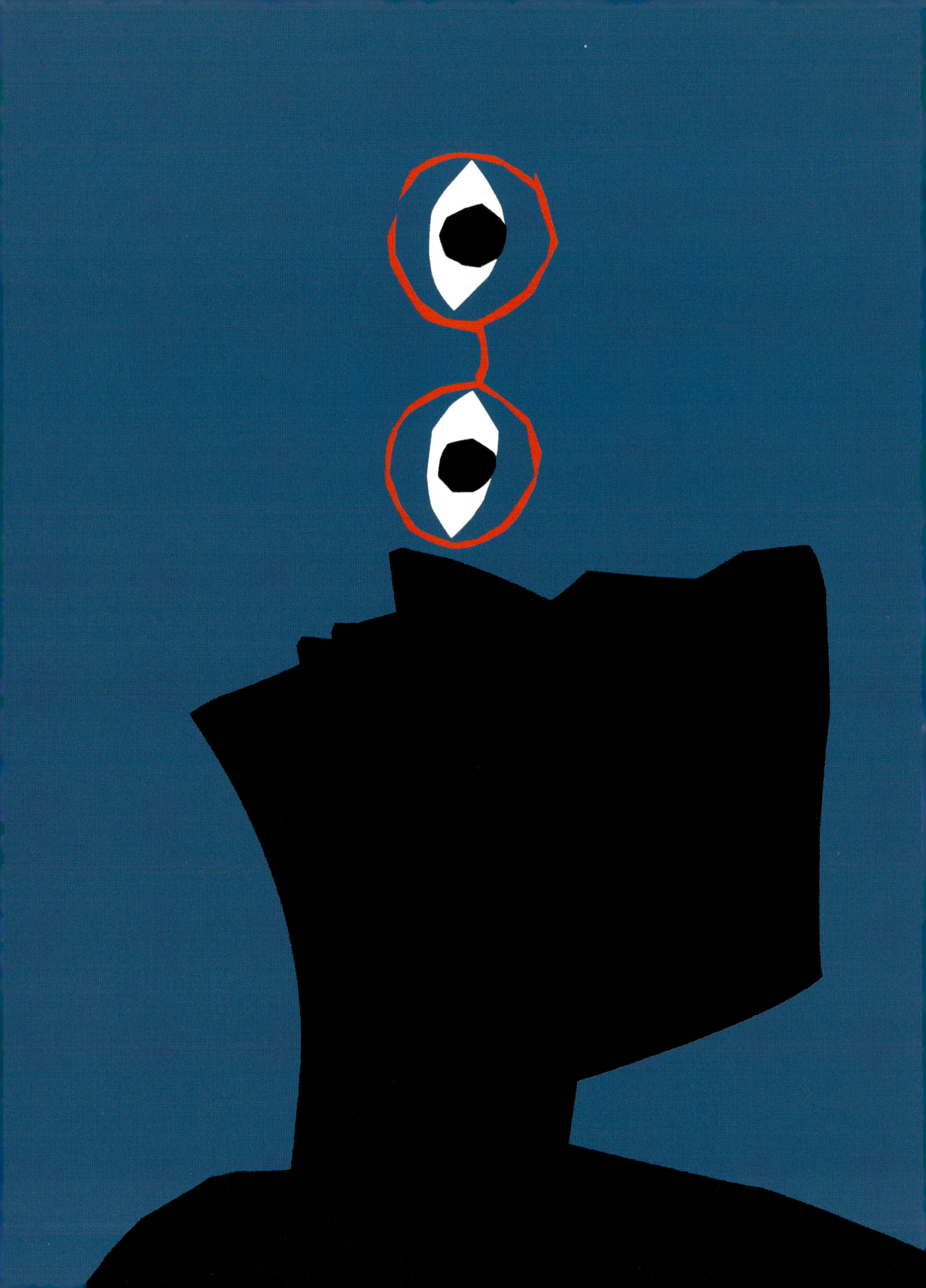

Cover for promotional brochure
Craig Frazier Studio, 1995

Editorial, *Summer Fiction*
Northeast magazine, 1996

Corporate collateral, *Sector investing*
Invesco Corporation, 2000

Corporate collateral, *A new approach*
Company Entier, 1997

Editorial, fiction issue
Northeast magazine, 1996

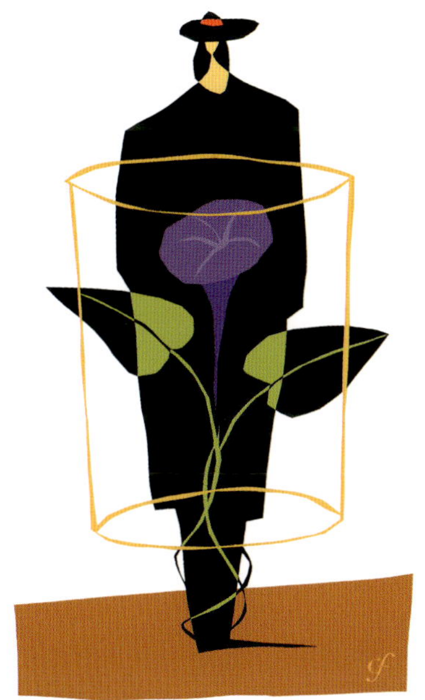

Collateral
Breast Center, 1996

Editorial, fiction issue
Northeast magazine, 1996

Editorial, fiction issue
Northeast magazine, 1997

Editorial, fiction issue
Northeast magazine, 1996

Poster/brochure, *Listening to the customer*
Oracle Computers, 1994

Poster/brochure, *Insight*
Oracle Computers, 1994

Ink and paper.

I had the good fortune of entering graphic design pre-computer, when we designed to print. It was a slow, analog process that taught me a particular reverence for the creation of ideas and their ultimate expression. Preparation for print took a long time by today's digital standards, but the benefit was a respect for the permanence of ink on paper.

In the '80s, this is how most reputable design firms initiated young designers. Regardless of their design chops, they'd have to learn design production—the non-creative tail end of the process. The dreams of designing a logo, art directing a photographer, or attending a client meeting were suspended until you earned your stripes assembling "mechanicals," making art "print-ready." Rubber cement, Rapidographs, non-repro blue pencils, type galleys, Amberlith, circle templates, triangles, and T-squares were the tools that either lived on your table or in the taboret beside you. There were good habits learned and bad habits quashed. The fate of a designer's work rested solely on the execution of this process. Accuracy was the name of the game. Poor craftsmanship or haste made for errors that could haunt you forever, because paper and ink never forget. Excelling in production was the only way to ensure your employment and prove your worthiness to advance to junior designer. Or prove otherwise.

We were very involved in the printing of our work from the selection of the printer to attending press checks. The '80s and '90s saw tremendous advancements in printing technology, and it was the best designers, photographers, and illustrators who would step up the industry's standards. The challenges lay in the reproduction of color, tone, and contrast—and ultimately the ability to faithfully reproduce the original art. These were all variables dependent on press technology, color separation, film work, paper, and ultimately the pressmen, presswomen, and behind-the-scenes craftsmen.

Companies were printing materials at a fever pitch. Annual reports, posters, brochures, catalogs, data sheets, and packages. Paper companies produced promotional literature like their lives depended on it—which they did. Printers fought ruthlessly for contracts, as riches awaited those who did the best work. Most often, exemplary printing was in service of exemplary design. Designers, photographers, and illustrators banked their reputations on how well their work looked in print. The food chain was never so apparent. The best illustrators were contracted by the best designers who had the best clients, and sent their work to the best printers. It became a blood sport.

The lessons of those times, the fundamentals of making lasting impressions, were indelible. The medium was physical and the experience was analog. The goal of the content was to suspend the turning of the page, to hold the reader's attention as long as possible. This applied to all printed matter. A business card was a handheld reason to remember you. An ad was a one-shot opportunity to speak with a potential customer one-on-one. A poster's job was to interrupt the landscape, and if lucky, wind up on a bedroom wall. Print was the medium designed explicitly to arrest the reader's attention for that precious moment—and hopefully create a memory. The connection of content to purpose was never more pure.

I consider it a gift to have trained in design during the heyday of print. My orientation is always "the page," and creating a connection with a reader—whether on paper or a device. Once the page is turned, the conversation is over.

The 1988 World's Most Memorable Poster
Jan 24 - Feb 8 Western Merchandise Mart

Abstraction grants great
liberties with execution.

Poster and bus shelter
San Francisco Conservation Corp, 1998

Corporate employee brochure
3Com Corporation, 1999

Collateral
US Postal Service, 1997

Editorial
Family Life Magazine, 1997

Editorial
The Boston Globe, 1999

Collateral and advertising
Invesco, 1999

Collateral
Imation, 1997

Collateral
Fremont Group, 1999

The wit's end.

In the beginning of my illustration career, I didn't feel that I drew that well, particularly compared to the standard-bearers of contemporary illustration. I couldn't paint and I was nervous about color. I lacked an established style. I had, however, drawn a lot of logos and pictographs as a designer. This probably contributed to my inclination toward graphic and simple forms. I suppose the proverb, "when life gives you lemons, make lemonade," applied here.

Aware that my rendering skills were my weak link, I put all of my energy into expressing ideas. I was trying to tell simple stories that would make someone scratch their head, maybe notice that something isn't quite right. I made the decision not to do realistic illustration but rather conceptual illustration—one that favored abstract and idiosyncratic thinking. I figured that if I could make my work smart enough from the start, I could buy some time to develop and improve my drawing chops.

Eventually, I become so immersed in idea-making that I completely forgot about my beginner anxiety. I didn't worry about proportion, anatomy, scale, or things like the size of my character's head. I believed that since the stories I drew were fictional, my portrayal of the contents could be too. Huge legs, no fingers, green skies, trees that looked like pears. All of these things were acceptable because they weren't intended to be representational. Rather, they were merely symbols in a narrative I wanted to tell. Their distortion was all part of me learning the language of wit.

On the surface, we think of wit as intelligent humor. Like seeing the banana peel that the pedestrian is about to slip on, not the obvious silliness that follows. But on a deeper level, we see wit in forms that resemble visual riddles, or incongruities that intrigue us and bear investigation. It's putting objects in places they don't belong, casting shadows into forms they don't resemble, exchanging what we expect to see with something contradictory, or stopping time at a moment that beckons us to predict the outcome in our heads. Wit is the welcome mat into the illustration, which begs the question, "what's going on here?"

The urge to incorporate wit in my work is out of appreciation for seeing it everywhere else in my life. I love to laugh and I love the satisfaction of feeling I get from clever repartee. Wit is a key ingredient in meaningful conversation, a more colorful way of seeing the world. It is a character trait I value in people, as it allows them to exchange ideas with a degree of elegant playfulness.

Ironically, wit becomes a more viable approach the more serious the context. It's very rare that I get an assignment that strikes me as humorous upon initial reading. In fact, many are painfully solemn. Often even boring. Those are the very jobs that require the illustration to lift the reader to a place words can't do alone. Thank god for wit.

There is no short answer for convincing the nervous client about the intrinsic merits of wit, or whether a particular illustration will pass the test. I never attempt to second-guess a client or their audience. Nor do I overstate the obvious just to make doubly sure they get it. I rely on my own sense of what is witty for guidance. Drawings that take the least amount of explaining usually work best, while those that take the most explaining usually fail. Making witty drawings ultimately amounts to a practiced intuition, a willing client and a belief that people are smarter than we think. It's a high-wire act that prefers no net.

Annual Report
Redwood Trust, 2000

< Collateral
EMC Corporation, 1996

In-store poster
Cole Haan, 1996

Conference poster
Seattle AIGA, 1998

AIGA DESIGN CAMP 1998

A guy walks into a bar.

It happened by accident. I sketched this guy a few times and liked something about him—his charming ordinariness. He seemed like Joe Human. Drawn with almost no detail, like expressions, fingers, or even eyes—the perfect stunt man to cast into unusual situations or conundrums. I didn't want you to get to know him, instead I wanted you to feel a sense of identification with his peculiar situations. I wanted to create enough detachment, as if you were looking at a still frame from a movie, while at the same time feeling a twinge of empathy. As to say, "that's happened to me," or "I wish that was me," or "I'm glad that's not me."

In the beginning, Mr. Human was basically a stick figure with nice clothes. His attire was designed out of the "graphic opportunity" it presented. In a black suit, he cut a simple silhouette that allowed for the slightest positioning of arms and legs to define his point of view or gesture. He rarely wears a tie because that's too fussy a detail—and frankly, too expected. Then there's his signature hat, his chapeau. Why? Maybe a nod to Magritte, maybe to avoid drawing hair, maybe just a bit of style that garners our instant respect for him. The best reason for the hat is that the angle of the brim defines the entire attitude of his tiny orb head. In a way, his perspective on his situation is actually defined by the hat. With the fewest strokes, I can render where his invisible eyes are looking and his level of participation. Does he see something unusual? Does he find his circumstance perplexing? Does he have the answers? Maybe all of those. What we know for sure is that he's a gentleman, an everyman—an ambassador of askew.

Over time, my fellow traveler has evolved in parallel with my own evolution, as I learned to draw with a more refined sense of proportion, scale, and definition of hands, feet, and head. None of this has been intentional. In fact, I have had to restrain myself from making him look too "correct." I have to remember my original premise to maintain our distance from him, to focus our eyes on the story he's telling.

Occasionally, he interacts with others, but most frequently he is independently observing and dealing with the world around him. We're unsure of his background, or even what era he's from. But we do know he represents no one in particular, because he represents everyone. He's got a bit part on the grand life stage—one we all can share every now and then.

Speaking poster
Meredith Corporation, 1997

Corporate employee brochure
3Com Corporation, 1999

Collateral
Nobix, 1999

CD cover, *Best of Times*
Supertramp, 1998

Corporate collateral
Harris Bank, 1997

In 1997, I sat drawing in my new studio over Peet's coffee, listening to Dylan's *Time Out of Mind* three times a day for a year. This was the job I was looking for.

—Bob Dylan, *Highlands*

Retail poster, packaging
Au Bon Pain, 1997

Editorial
Stanford Magazine, 2001

Collateral, *Our executive team*
Redwood Trust, 2006

I want to leave just enough signals
so that a viewer can find a story
that means something to them.

Editorial, *Breast Cancer*
Herman Hospital Magazine, 2000

Editorial
Attaché magazine, 2000

Poster
AidsWalk, San Francisco, 1998

98 AIDS Walk SF

Corporate collaeral/branding
Invesco, 1999

Collateral, *Built for people*
Company Entier, 1997

Editorial, *Managing oneself*
Harvard Business Review, 1999

Collateral
Swieter Design, 1998

Editorial
Reader's Digest, 2001

Editorial illustration, *Healing italy*
Time, 2001

Brochure illustration, *Global banking*
Mastercard, 1997

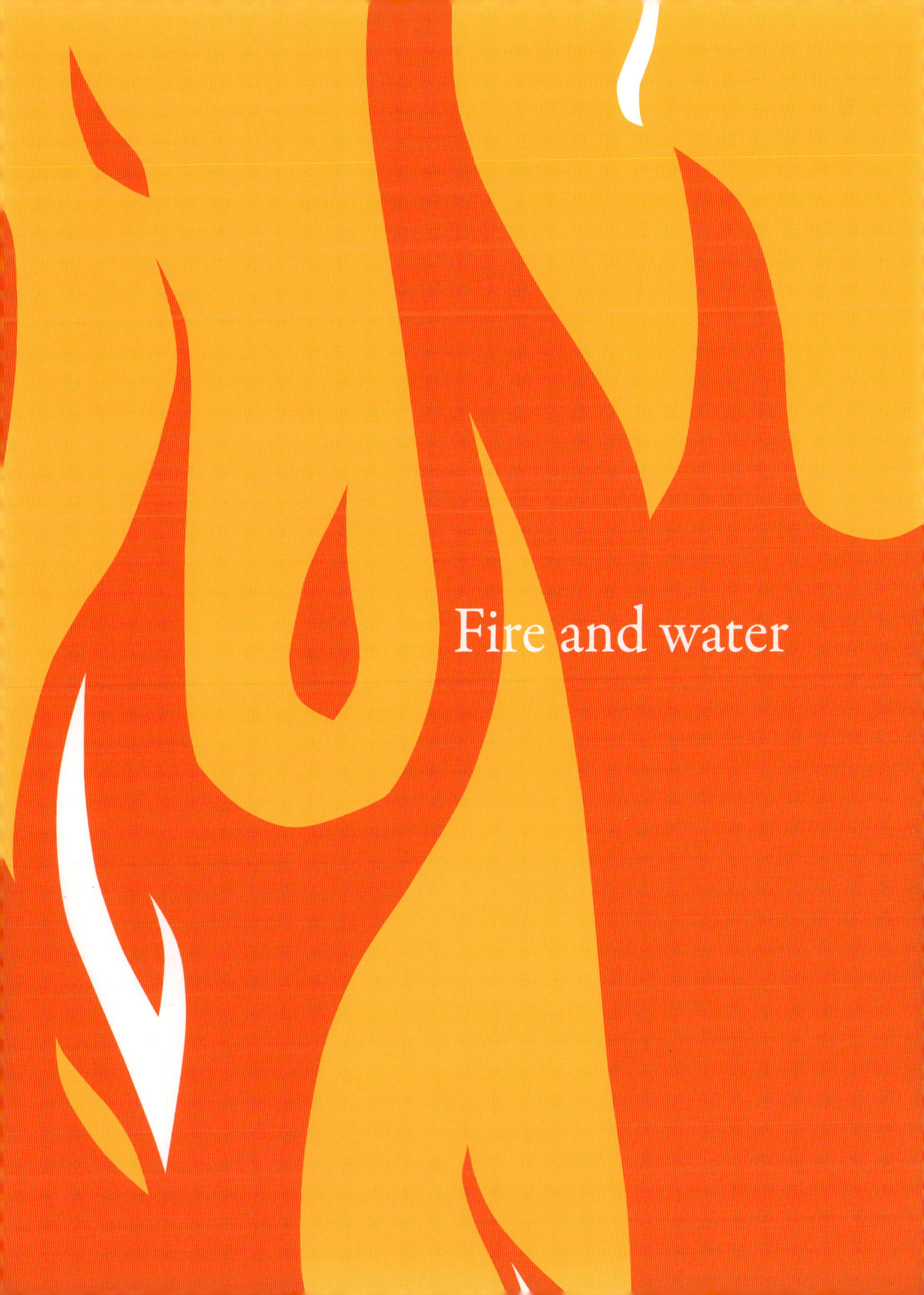
Fire and water

Poster
Santa Cruz Guitar Company, 2002

SANTA CRUZ
GUITAR COMPANY
frazier

Colleague remarks.

Steven Heller
Author, Critic
Craig Frazier, master of conceptual style, has defined American illustration for over thirty years. *Drawn* proves that his approach is as fresh today as when he began.

Ivan Chermayeff
Designer
I like to think that one of the explanations for Craig's expressive and memorable illustrations is that he has been, and still is, a designer. The search for a concept, and not putting anything down until a concept is found, is what makes the end product great work that communicates—often about difficult subjects.

To get provocative and meaningful end results requires a grasp of the essential ingredients, knowledge about what they are, and the intelligence to exploit them. Scale, surprise, observation, and subtle shifts are the hallmarks of Craig's illustrations. He knows what he's doing.

The continuous outpouring of excellence is never an accident. On the contrary, Craig's hard work and intelligence is omnipresent.

Joe Morse
Illustrator, Educator
At the heart of Craig's work is drawing—the serious business of putting pen to paper. He draws in a language that rewards curiosity, challenges conformity, and welcomes contradiction. I would make *Drawn* a textbook in every illustration school in the world!

Christoph Neimann
Illustrator
To be a successful illustrator you need 70 points. To be Craig Frazier you need 100 points.

You get 10 points for the ability to spend ungodly amounts of time in front of a white piece of paper, and not lose your spirit when most of your ideas don't work.

You get 30 points for refusing to give up; for trying to succeed by merging those ideas into something new, only to find that ninety-nine percent of them don't work either; steadfastly refusing to translate a headline into an image; fighting against editors trying to translate your image into a headline.

You get 30 points if you do all of the above every day, every week, every month, ideally for a couple of decades.

You get the last 30 points only if you actually are Craig Frazier. Sorry.

Personal
Craig Frazier, 2004

Kit Hinrichs

Designer

Craig is a very rare individual. He can capture the most serious of subjects with grace, humor, and humility.

Arriving here from New York in the late '70s, I was welcomed by a group of artists and designers, including a young Craig Frazier, whose work I admired. I identified with their notable personal styles and craftsmanship. Most of them had an elegance, a unique color palette, a graphic boldness, and an identifiable visual technique in their work—which collectively created the rich, distinctive tapestry that defined San Francisco Bay Area design.

Craig stood apart from that illustrious group. His images had all the markings of a designer with a "singular visual language," but what separated him from the pack was his unique vision of the world. It wasn't style alone that fueled his success, it was his always-arresting ideas.

Craig's endless visual concepts combined with his dusty dry wit and wordplay continue to demonstrate his rare intelligence, curious mind, and deep pool of intrinsic talent—all of which he has generously shared with us through the years. He has enriched our lives and enhanced the value of the design profession. I am proud to call him a colleague and good friend.

Michael Schwab

Designer, Illustrator

Craig Frazier's graphic work takes us to a distant and unique place—a thoughtful plateau with intriguing deceptions and illusions. No rules of gravity or perspective exist here, yet it's calm and peaceful. A lesson in life? Maybe. It's always worth the trip.

Ken Segall

Creative Director, Author

As agency lead on Apple in LA, I once enthusiastically sent a great candidate for our team north to get Steve Jobs's blessing. He rejected her outright. "She wasn't curious. She didn't ask questions. Smart people are curious," he said. Brutal, but true.

Steve would have loved Craig. He is the poster boy for curiosity. He's like a child the way he picks up an idea, rolls it around like a toy, pokes it from every angle, unafraid to break it in the process. And when he's not breaking things, you can talk to him like the wonderfully wise adult he is. I don't know what makes me smile more—Craig's visual wit, or his ability to compress so much insight, human and strategic, into such little space.

Karin Hibma Cronan

Principal of CRONAN

Craig's talent in design—and later his relentless focus on expressing big ideas through imagery—always adds a perfectly pitched note. The one that makes you remember almost wistfully the moment, the insight, the aha, the sense of knowing. What a gift this compendium of work and insights is!

Kirk Citron
Writer, Creative Director
Craig writes with visuals. Where most illustrators draw objects or people, he draws ideas. This means the virtues of his work are the virtues of good writing: poetry, wit, metaphor.

It's not just that he has a distinctive style—it's that his style is in service to a broader understanding of how people look at images, how they react, how they take things in.

He thinks like the designer he is. As a result, he has pushed the field of illustration in new directions. When you see his forty-plus-year body of work in one place, it's impossible not to appreciate his singular contribution to contemporary illustration.

Richard Danne
Designer
Simply put, Craig is one of the most gifted creative people I've ever known.

It all starts with his Intelligence Quotient. Craig has an IQ that comes through in each and every piece he creates. He thinks things through from every possible angle before he ever renders a finished product. He is relentless and digs until he finds the most beautiful, surprising, and imaginative solution possible.

At his core, Craig is a true designer. He's a problem-solver, and his solutions are always deeper and more satisfying than those of most good illustrators. Finally, of course, there is the finished graphic image —always excellent, always a cut above, and clearly recognizable as Craig Frazier.

Paul Rogers
Ilustrator, Educator
I've admired Craig's work for decades and it's great to see the collection together, to read his thoughts about process and the business of illustration. I show his work to my students as examples of the best conceptual thinking in illustration.

Emiliano Ponzi
Illustrator
In 2000, as a young Italian illustrator, I used to look at American masters in the annuals. That's when I discovered Craig Frazier. I could easily recognize a clarity of intention that is more common in graphic designers than illustrators. It's a gift to have a book containing such a massive number of his images, sketches, and handmade artworks in order to fully appreciate his artistry.

Antonio Castro
Designer, Educator
I continually insist that my students aim for smart and beautiful solutions. Getting there requires curiosity, tenacity, passion, and work. This is what *Drawn* is all about. It not only shows the vast amount of great work that Craig has produced for over forty years, but also shares his arduous and fruitful process.

Editorial illustration, *The Puzzle Issue*
The New York Times, 2010

European advertising, *Partners in space*
Boeing, 2004

Editorial
Strategy + Business magazine, 2009

Buried treasures.

Sometimes the solution comes quickly, sometimes it simply takes forever. A possible explanation is that one topic might seem inherently more interesting than another, inspiring more immediate possibilities. For instance, a jazz festival (page 233) might conjure more stimulating images than an article explaining "asset acquisition" (opposite page). Both assignments trigger different responses at different speeds. The "festival" looks easy because the words offer visual clues and it is a familiar event, but therein lies the trap. I don't always trust my instant solutions. In fact, I'm suspicious of them. If the solution appears too quickly, it may also occur quickly to the viewer, which means it may not be novel after all.

On the other hand, illustrating "asset acquisition"— seemingly more difficult at first glance—actually presents more opportunities for invention. Because we are less informed about the subject, most of us start with fewer preconceptions, so the possibility for abstract concepts are more available. For me, this kind of assignment leads to visual metaphors and surreal scenarios—cobbling together familiar symbols to tell a new story. It becomes the perfect place to use irony, wit, and juxtaposition to create a new porthole into a subject. If I'm intrigued by my solution, I'm pretty sure you will be.

This was a big discovery, as it means that sometimes the scariest assignments are actually the richest. My unfamiliarity with a subject has actually opened a window into more provocative solutions. It taught me to turn fear into curiosity into opportunity.

My goal is always to get a little further "out there," which requires exploring the obvious first, then digging deeper. This may be the most challenging part of illustrating, but it is the required work and it does, in fact, reward you. It's like finding that fabulous T-shirt buried beneath the ones you wear every day.

Turns out I gained a reputation for these kinds of assignments, which would attract other clients, particularly in the financial world. They have complex issues that need to be explained in terms we all can understand—and hopefully learn from.

By the way, jazz posters are a lot harder to design than they look!

Annual report
Orion Capital, 2000

I'm drawn to incongruity. It's like the hair out of place that you can't stop staring at.

Corporate collateral
Support Tech, Inc., 1998

Collateral
Unifund, 2006

Editorial
How magazine, 2001

Paper swatchbooks, *Royal line*
Wausau Paper Company, 1999

Poster, *Royal Silk*
Wausau Paper Company, 1999

Paper swatchbook
Wausau Paper Company, 1999

Editorial, *Summer Movies*
Los Angeles Times, 2010

Editorial, *Film Festival*
Los Angeles Times, 2002

Dollars and sense.

We hope that practice leads to improvement, while understanding that the process is typically slow and steady, and results are often subtle. There are, however, occasions where a tiny shift in process makes a tangible change.

Certain illustrations stand out because they lead to breakthroughs, though entirely unintentional at the time. This is one of them. I did a couple of things differently.

The first was the attitude of the illustration in response to the editorial content. This *Harvard Business Review* article was about executives' view of pay—the fact that most of them believed in out-of-date myths and were generally out of sync with the times. The article was highly critical.

I presented a drawing that I felt reflected the author's frank and cynical sentiment. I found his style of writing honest and easy to draw to. He was poking, so I had license to do the same.

The figure stands with arms crossed, looking straight ahead, his view shrouded by two dollar bills tied to his head. He seems focused and fixed in his body language—presenting a certain stubborn arrogance. This mere fabrication tells us it's an absurd scenario, while at the same time sending its biting message.

The second breakthrough was in the drawing itself. Since I am always trying to be as simple and graphic as possible, I wrestle with the level of detail a drawing will have. Up to this point, I had been confining myself to very flat silhouettes that tended to be drawn either head-on or in profile.

In this case, I needed to draw the figure in more of a three-quarter view in order to better describe his crossed arms and reveal the perspective of the second dollar bill. I realized that if I could incorporate the slightest bit of line work, I could add significantly more information and provoke more interest.

I was inspired by Picasso's drawings of seated men—how his line so fluidly described the folds in their clothes' fabric. A single line employed to create form plus volume.

I worked from one of my sketches and tried to maintain its gesture and style, while remaining true to its simplicity. Every element had to be drawn with no greater detail than the next. I distilled the design of the dollar bill to its barest essentials—too much information would be distracting. By making the lines in his coat dark gray, the boldness of the overall figure is not sacrificed. The string is red so it draws just the right amount of attention. The man's hands are as minimal as possible. Two ivory triangles define the openings in his single-button coat.

Content and form in harmony. I often refer to this illustration to remind me of its simple recipe: appropriate doses of idea, attitude, and execution. No more, no less.

Editorial, Op/ed
The New York Times, 2006

Editorial, Op/ed
The New York Times, 2001

Editorial, Op/ed
The New York Times, 2000

Editorial, *E-shopping Failures*
Wall Street Journal, 2002

Corporate editorial
Trust magazine, Baillie Gifford, 2021

Editorial, *Growth Crisis*
Harvard Business Review, 2002

Advertising, *Fun in, Fun out*
Chevrolet, 1999

Corporate collateral, *Networking*
Support Tech, Inc., 1998

I look for clues in the story.
If it's about computers, I
usually start drawing plants.

Collateral
USI Consulting Group, 1998

Laws of attraction.

Amongst the various requirements of assignment work lies the most difficult—to make the drawing interesting. In fact, quite often we are asked to make uninteresting topics interesting to those who aren't typically interested. It's a mind-bending exercise at the core of almost every assignment that lands on my drawing board.

What is interesting? One person's interesting is another's boring. One person's mundane is another's stimulating. It's profoundly subjective. It's not taught in schools, nor is it typically brought up by clients, but they all want it in the end. It's intangible, which makes it undefinable, yet it's the linchpin of a good piece of work.

What's interesting is often the very reason we like something. It's the invitation to a conversation. If we're not interested, the conversation never starts. The entire business of design relies on our ability to create interest. It's ironic that making something interesting can appear so elusive, and that the punishment for failing to do so can be so dramatic. Pages are turned, ads passed by, books unopened, emails scrolled past, websites clicked through, images tarnished and money lost—all due to lack of interest. Dismissal is a light that doesn't get turned on.

Time is limited and we can't afford to be uninterested. Conversely, being interested is the gatekeeper for our attention, our time, and our quest to learn. It's like chocolate for the curious—the reward is coming back for more. I have always believed intuitively that for my work to be successful, I had better make it interesting.

Ad agencies and marketing firms often take the pulse of their intended audience's interest through polls and focus groups, then build design and products to fit the bill. All in the effort to calculate and program creativity. Great companies work inversely. They make interesting, often genius products, and turn customers on to them.

I've never tried to second-guess my clients or their audiences. My job is to interest you in what I'm interested in drawing.

Editorial
Wink magazine, 2000

You can't force a style—
it arrives when it's ready.

Corporate collateral
MasterCard Advisors, 2004

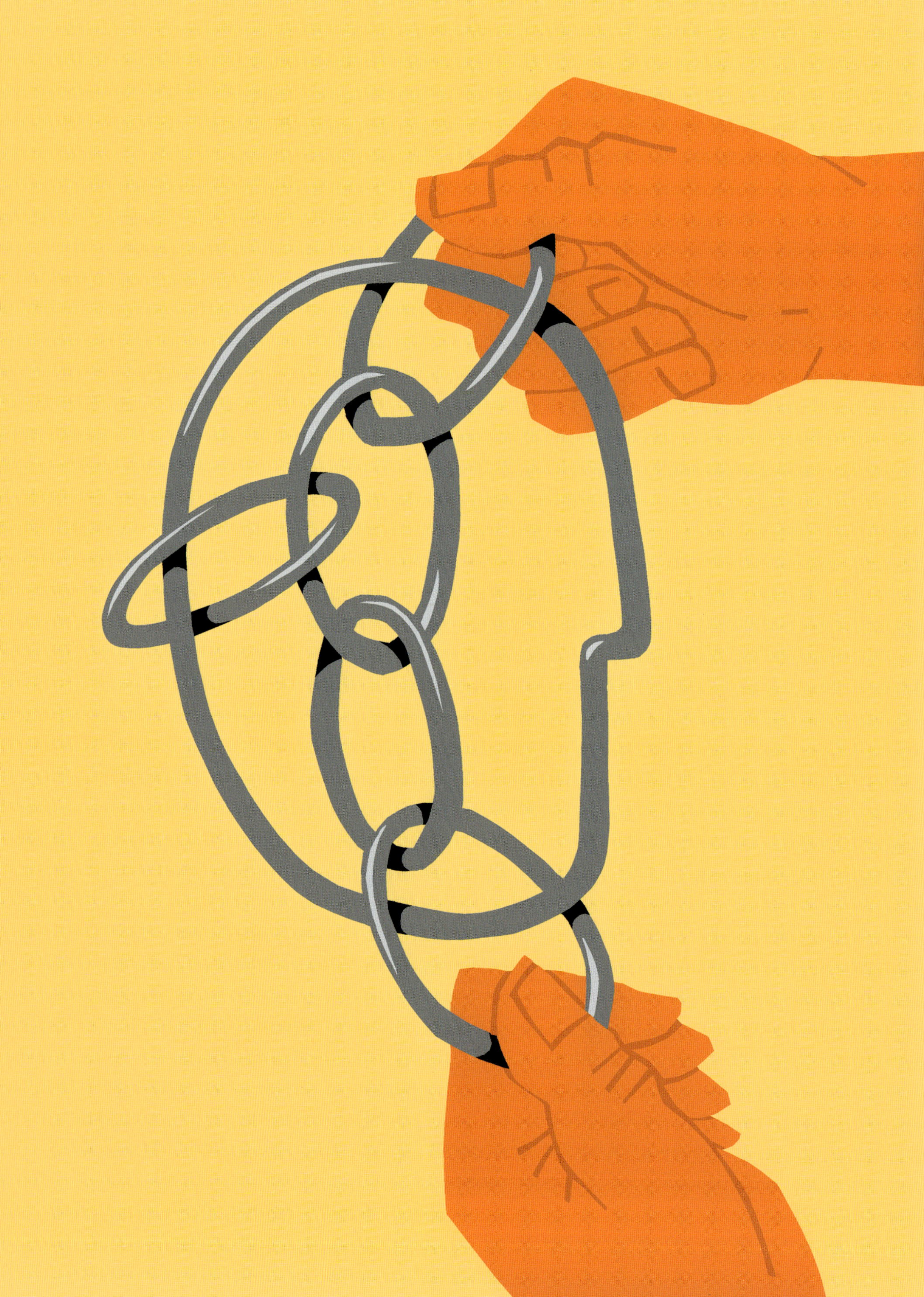

Editorial
Yale Alumni magazine, 2003

Book cover
Hampton Roads Publishing, 2000

Collateral
Support Tech, Inc., 1998

Poster/animation
Adobe, 2001

By hand

Turning over stones.

If this job bears any stresses, they are born of the business side. Being creative is only made stressful by deadlines, imposed restraints, and difficult clients. The actual work of illustrating is two-part—a hunting exercise looking for the right answer to a problem, and the pleasure of making the finished art. The daily routine of putting pen to paper to find a solution is transportive in ways that we struggle to replicate. When we are in a groove, it's easy to feel like an observer of a magic performance. Most of the time.

As a young designer, I knew that graphic design was a problem-solving job. It wasn't decoration, it wasn't art, it was about finding an expression that was custom-fit to solve a client's problem. My earliest years were spent in an honest pursuit, to find the one right solution. This proved to be both frustrating for me and a difficult business practice. Eventually, I changed and a pressure valve was opened. I realized there is rarely only one right answer. There may be several. Perhaps counter-intuitively, finding multiple solutions did not make the job more complicated. Rather, it provided a new sense of freedom.

For every finished illustration, there are dozens of preparatory sketches that will never go beyond their line on paper—they are the long-lost cousins in an illustration's family tree.

I have maintained the "multiple solution" approach my entire illustration career. With this process, several things can happen. When you abandon the single-solution tact, you are liberated to "walk around the problem." This leads to expanding the horizon of ideas. It sustains a state of ideation and suspension of judgment for a longer time—which means more ideas. It's the opposite process of going down a single rabbit hole that, in fact, may not lead to the best solution at all. To focus on creating one

solution only narrows the funnel. It rushes you to the tail of the process before there is a lot to choose from. The fact is that multiple solutions reveal myriad vantage points from which a problem can be viewed. Oftentimes I will develop a couple of solid solutions, which give me the liberty to think outside the given definition of the problem. As a result, I may discover something that supports a redefinition of the challenge. Discovery can't be truncated. Some of my most interesting ideas arrive at the moment I'm about to put my pen down.

As a conceptual illustrator, my drawings aren't intended to be depictive of a reality, rather they are in search of an idea that offers a new perspective. This kind of exercise is a type of semi-conscious meandering—turning over stones until something appears. It's a conversation between mind and hand, mining for that moment when absurdity collides with purpose. It's only with years of practice that I have begun to trust that this simple process will be fruitful if I stick with it long enough. It is tireless, and not optional, if the job is to make illustrations that contribute wit and meaning to the designed world.

I don't show my clients all of my exploratory sketches. I do, however, show them a choice of two or three ideas per commission. They seem to appreciate this approach. Even though I'm not inviting collaboration into the ideation process, I am inviting the client into a 360-degree examination of their problem. This simple idea of choice tends to change the dynamic to "which one of the solutions does the job best." Sometimes a solution will inspire a client to redefine the message to fit more comfortably with that solution. Magically, the conversation moves from the pressure of a finished product to a world of expansive ideas— generally beyond their expectation. This is the basis for both good work and good business.

Sketches and color presentation illustrations
*sketch inspired the 2006 Love stamp (page 237)
**Final "Nurturing Love" envelope
US Postal Service, 2003

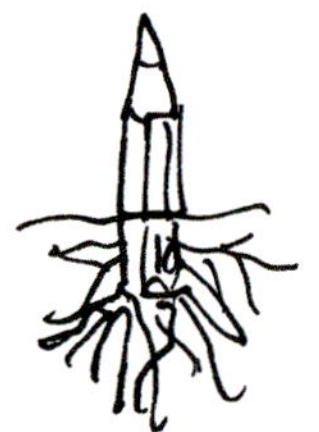

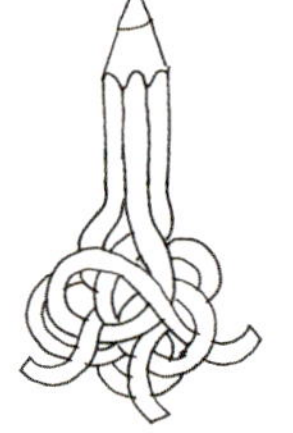

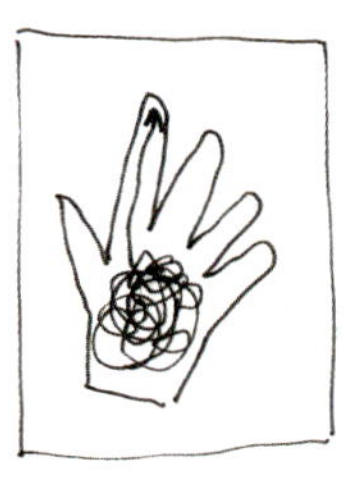

Think
Simple
How Smart Leaders
Defeat Complexity
New York Times bestselling
author of Insanely Simple
Ken Segall

Think Simple
How Smart Leaders
Defeat Complexity
Ken Segal New York Times bestselling author of Insanely Simple

How Smart
Leaders
Defeat
Complexity
Think
Simple
KEN SEGALL

Think Simple
How Smart Leaders Defeat Complexity
KEN SEGALL

Book cover sketches, mock-ups, and final cover
Think Simple by Ken Segall
Penguin Random House, 2016

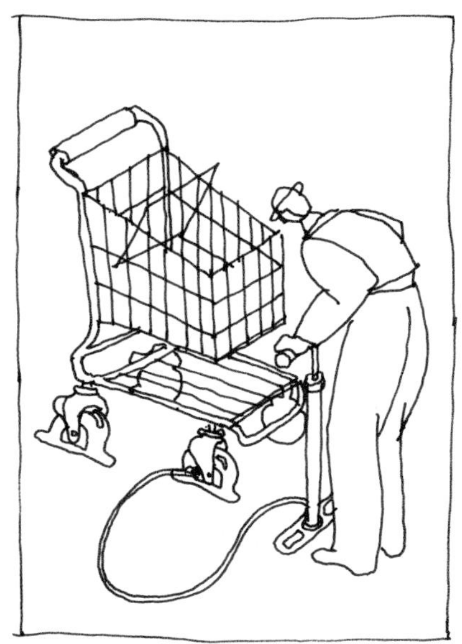

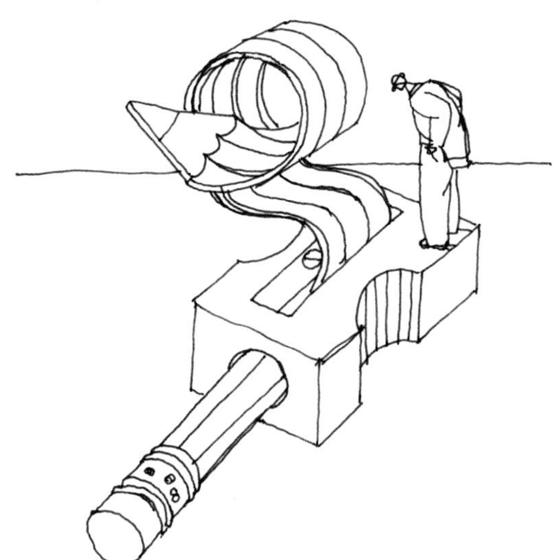

MADE IN USA

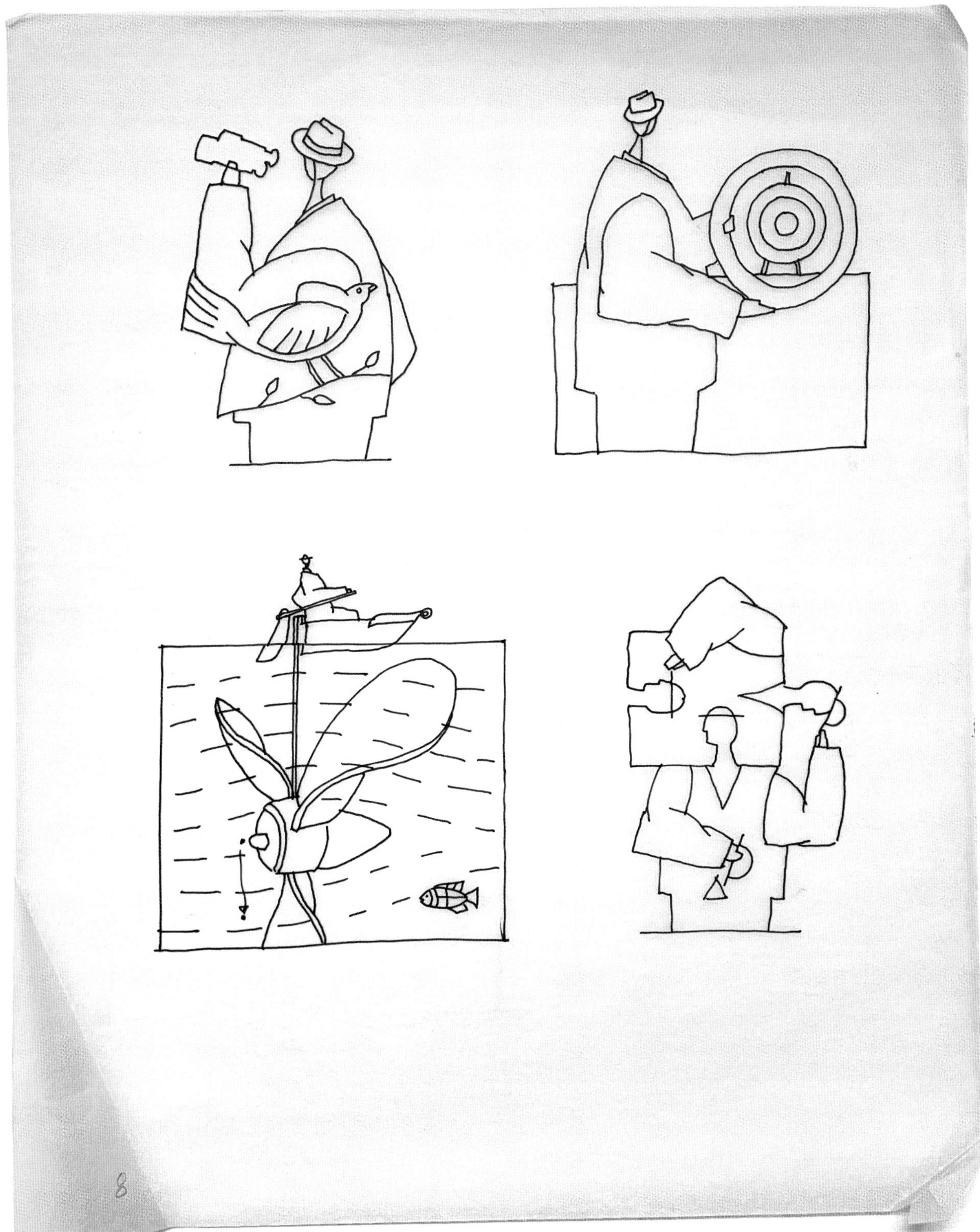

Sketching is like listening
with your eyes.

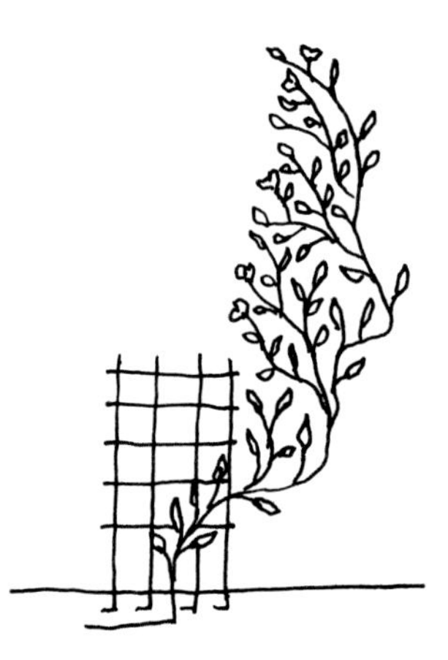

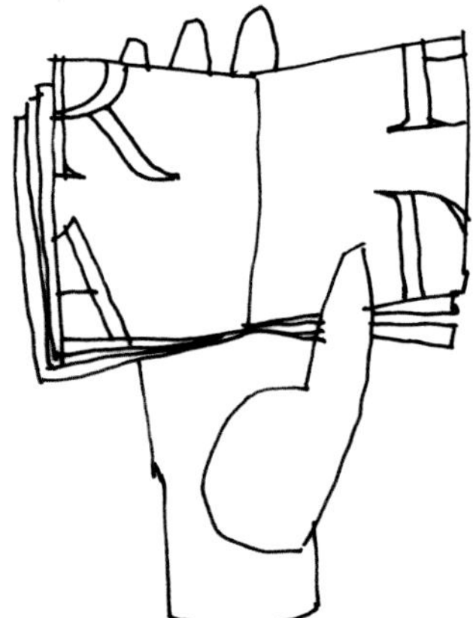

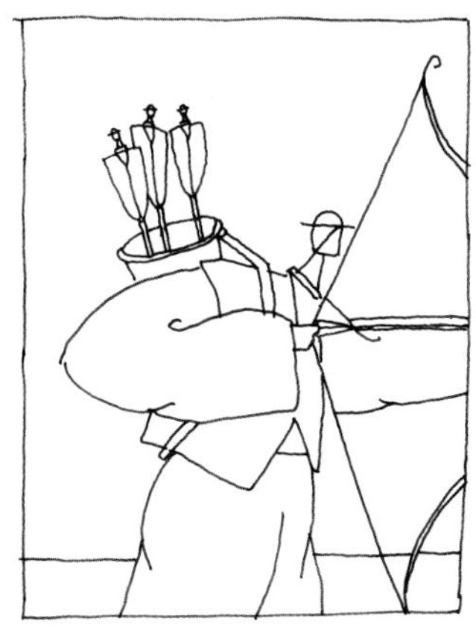

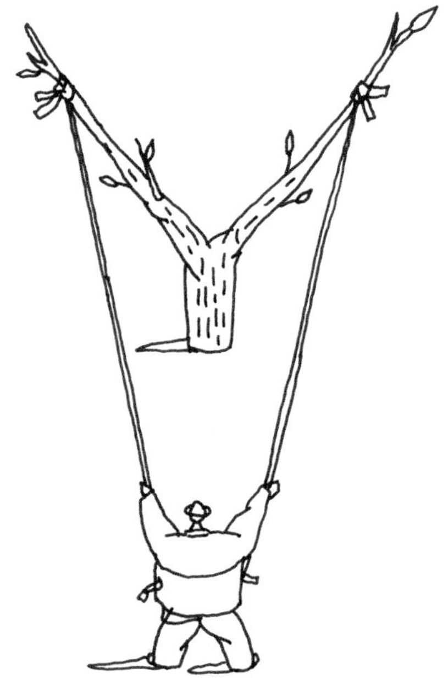

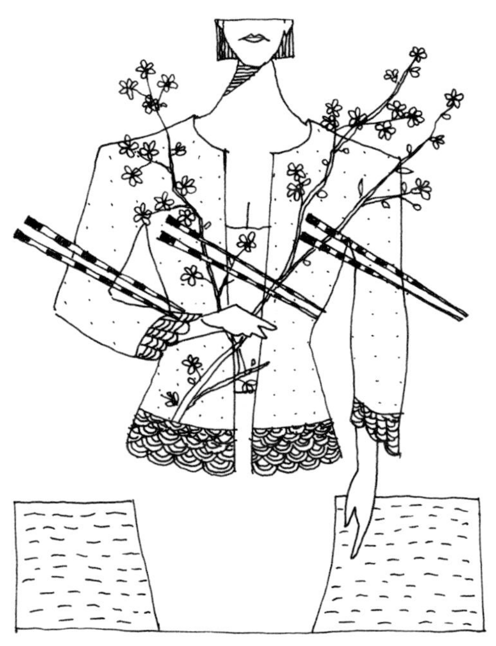

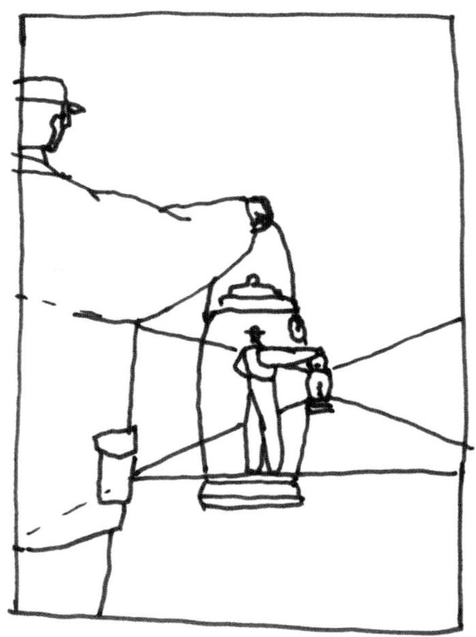
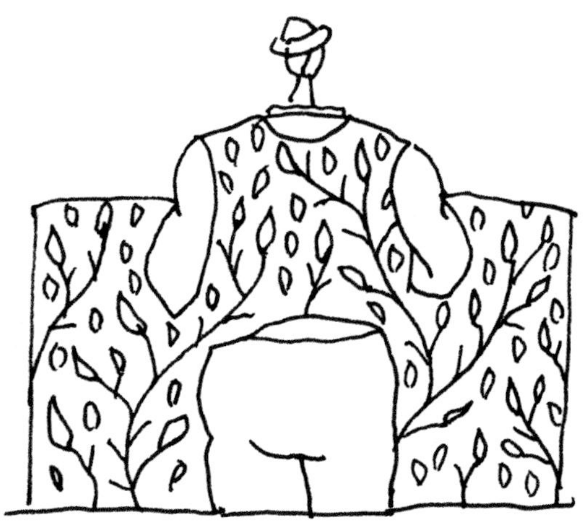

Inexact science.

If you were a designer in the pre-digital era, hand skills were a requisite for the job. The materials and tools available would shape not only the way you worked, but what your work looked like.

In 1980, the red masking film known as Amberlith was an essential tool in any design studio. Its primary role was to create "knockouts" for photographs or illustrations when producing art boards for printing. When cut with an Exacto knife, it would render a mask with a crisp and defined edge. Good eyes and a steady hand were not optional.

The more complex the subject's form, the more challenging the mask was to cut. Today, Photoshop can do this in a matter of minutes—stripping away unwanted backgrounds like magic. A technical skill more than a manual one. However, pre-Photoshop, if we wanted a ballet dancer lifted from the stage, her form was only as well defined as our Exacto blade could cut. Not everyone liked the job, but I did. It would serve as training for what would become a signature nuance of my illustration.

As I began to make the switch from designer to illustrator in the mid '90s, I started to draw with an Exacto knife. Initially, I was cutting out colored Pantone papers (page 35) and spray-mounting them down to board, scanning, and touching up in the early versions of Photoshop. There were myriad complications in this process and I soon realized it was unsustainable. I needed a quicker, cleaner, and more precise media to cut.

Fairly quickly, I found Amberlith to be the perfect solution. It's so good, I still use it twenty years later.

The technical benefits are resounding. Because the material is translucent, I can lay it on a sketch and cut as if I am tracing. I can cut multiple layers if I have forms that overlap and need to be registered. If I make a mistake, I can just cut another or repair in the computer. Because it is not colored paper, I am essentially making a monochromatic drawing that I will color in the computer—thus suspending my coloring commitments at this stage—cutting only with the intention of defining form.

The most significant feature of cutting Amberlith is the result. Unlike vector programs that are designed for accurate geometry and perfect curves, hand-cutting renders flaws that I find desirable. I purposely cut small (four to eight inches in height), forcing a limitation to detail and, in essence, a degree of imperfection. I welcome the accidents that come with drawing with a knife. It also becomes a built-in editor and keeps the illustration free of superfluous nuance—exactly what I am striving for. In the pursuit of simplicity, this is yet another tool in the elimination of unnecessary information. Side note: as a rule, I never cut one part of the illustration at one size and another part at a larger size to allow for more detail, then recompose in the computer. The eye knows the difference. The vocabulary of the entire piece must be consistent to be believable.

Did I invent this process? No, it's just another version of Henri Matisse's cut paper or the posters of Ivan Chermayeff, or the woodblock prints of the Japanese master printers. The goal is an elegant clarity of representation, just enough information but never too much. As time-consuming as it may appear, it's a very efficient means to an end. Once my ideas are worked out in pen, this is the foundational step in production of the final art. Between impending deadlines and my own impatience, it's a method that never disappoints.

ROLL

There's nothing like drawing with a knife. It forbids unnecessary detail —decisions get made for me.

My back pages.

I can't imagine approaching a project in design or illustration without the benefit of a habit I formed early on—working in a sketchbook. When I draw in a sketchbook, I feel like I'm making room in my head, like moving stuff from the dining room table to the garage. It permits a certain aimless visual wandering with no particular destination. No creative brief, no rules, no deadline, no judgment. It's a perfect place for conducting tests and storing pieces of ideas.

Occasionally I work on assignments in my sketchbook, but much of the time I'm just drawing with no end game in mind. Yet, strangely enough, the sketchbook is remarkably practical for the job of an illustrator. It is a research lab containing experiments often unfinished and inconclusive. What makes it so productive is that it houses these records of disparate musings made without expectation—each one adding to a catalogue of possibilities. A sketchbook allows a certain fearlessness to arise. Things happen over time, what once was an aimless doodle collides with another random sketch, and suddenly an idea is born. It's a repetitious journaling that pays off when you least expect it. Keith Richards didn't go to bed with the assignment to write a hit song, but he awakened to jot down the three-note riff that would one day become *Satisfaction*.

Much of the content of my sketchbook is a mystery to me, and that's a good thing. Sketching is an analog process, yet one of the most useful ways to elevate our work. With the simplest of tools, we can create realities from nothing and pose "what-ifs" with only a few lines. Sketches are the shorthand between problem and solution, designer and client, imagined and real. They are the work behind the work.

Ultimately, they represent a trove of half-baked ideas —sort of a garage full of parts waiting for a car to fix.

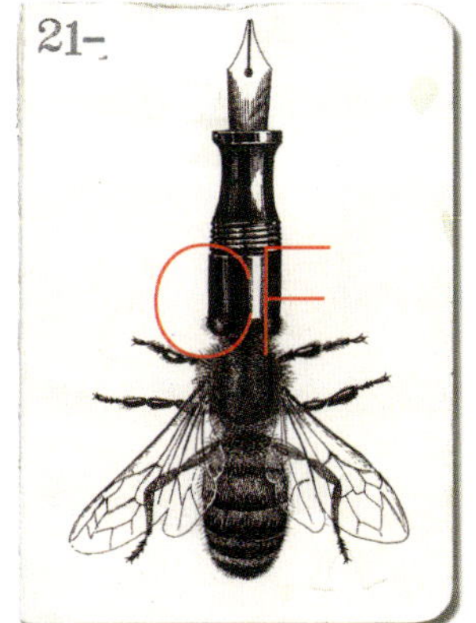

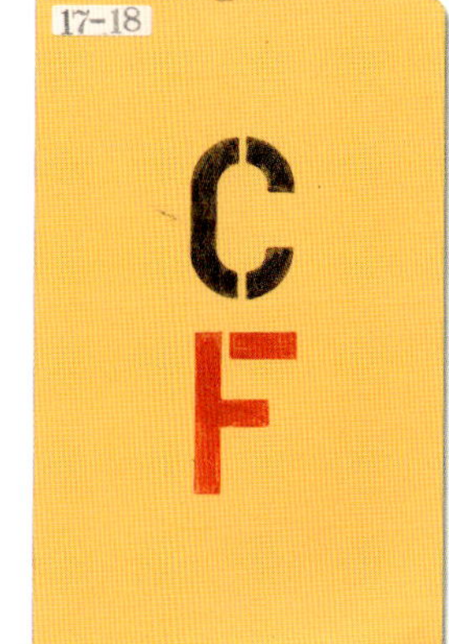

Sketchbooks, 1993-2023

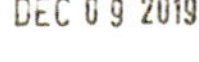

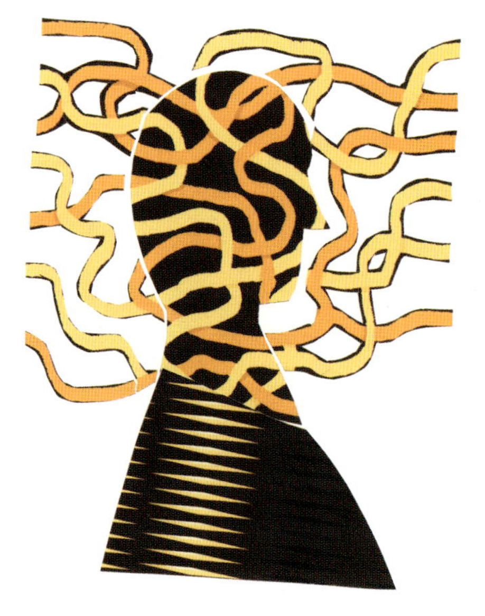

Sketchbooks, 1997–2023

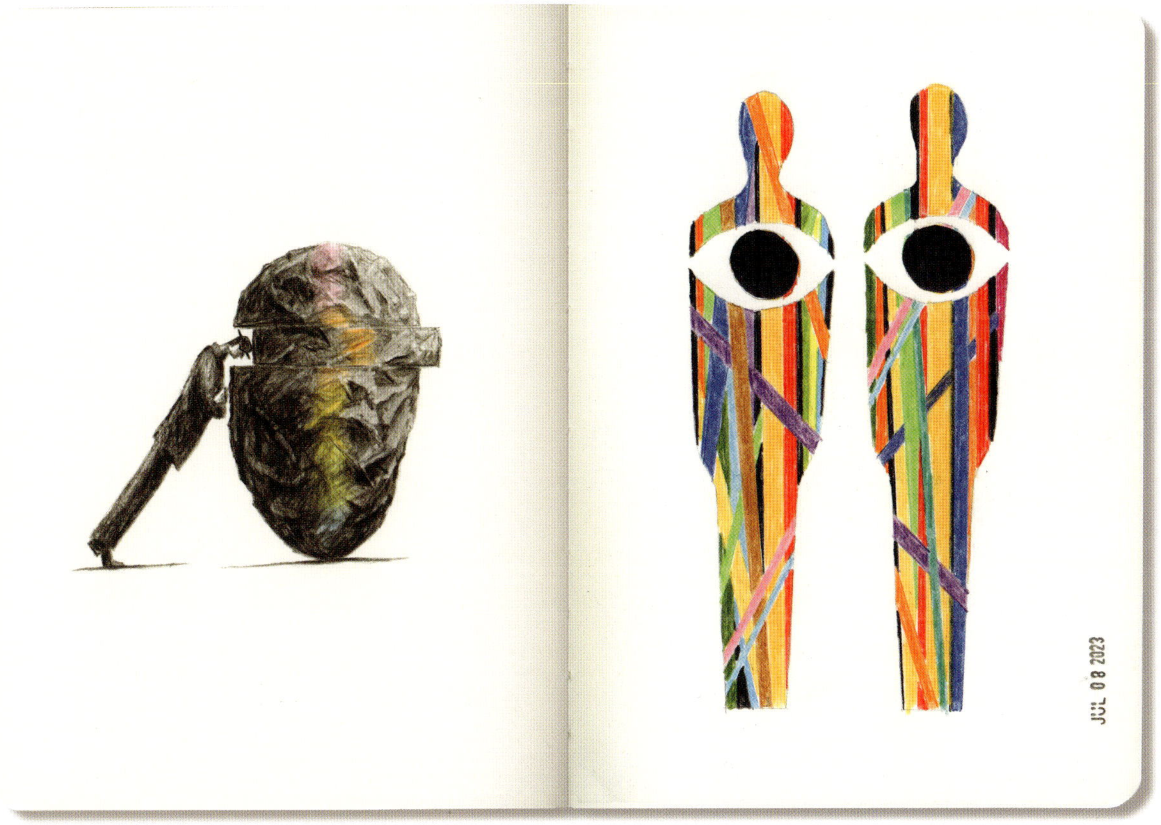

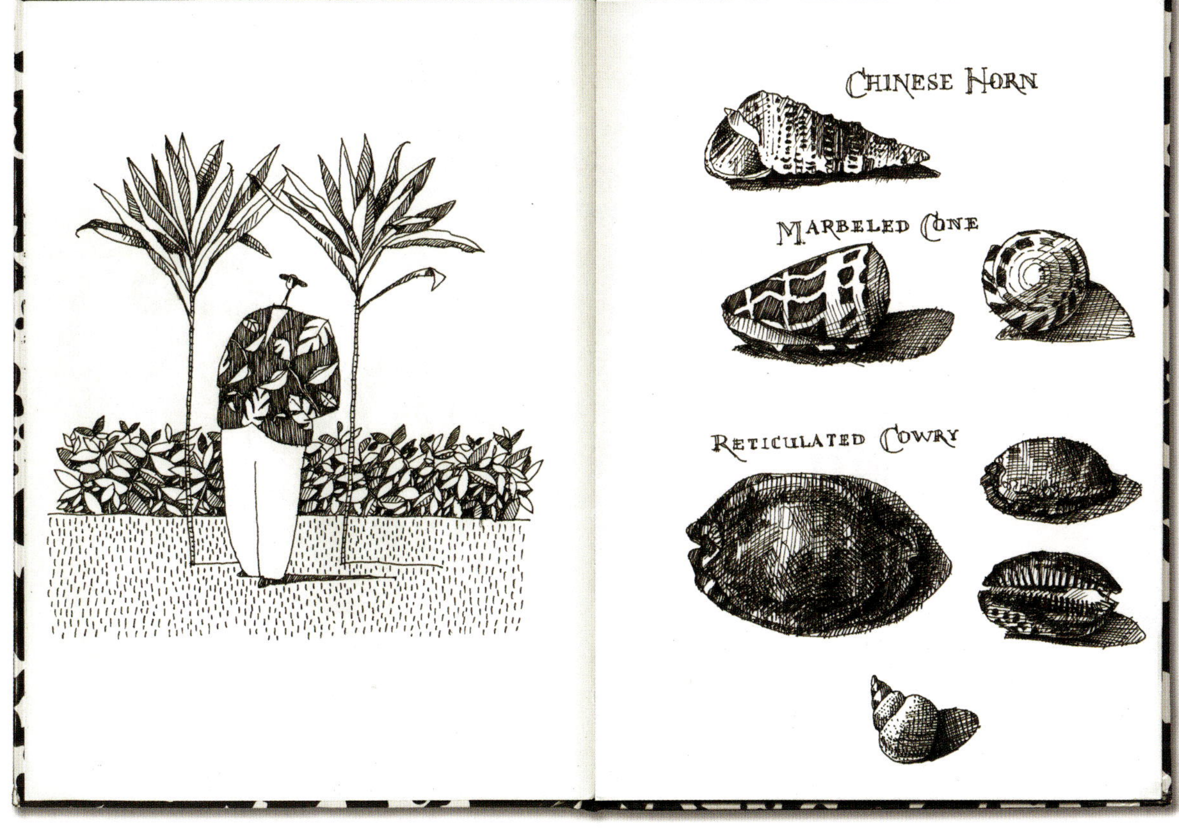
CHINESE HORN
MARBELED CONE
RETICULATED COWRY

APR 26 2021

SEP 10 2022
NORTHERN FLICKER TAIL FEATHER
DRAWN 2X ACTUAL SIZE

AMSTERDAM   10:00 AM   5.23.19

AMSTERDAM   5.24.19

COMB
DUCK
PIG
BRUSH
LEG
PEPPER
MOUSE
CAT
CUP
GUITAR
ARM
DRUM
SAUCER
SALT

4.25.13
MAN
HOUSE
RABBIT
FORK
FOX
BOAT
TABLE
WOMAN
SPOON
CAR
CHAIR
HAT
TIE
TREE
HEN
EGG

OCT 0 9 2022

PEKIN DUCK TAIL FEATHER
KINDERHOOK FARMS
VALATIE, NEW YORK 10.4.22

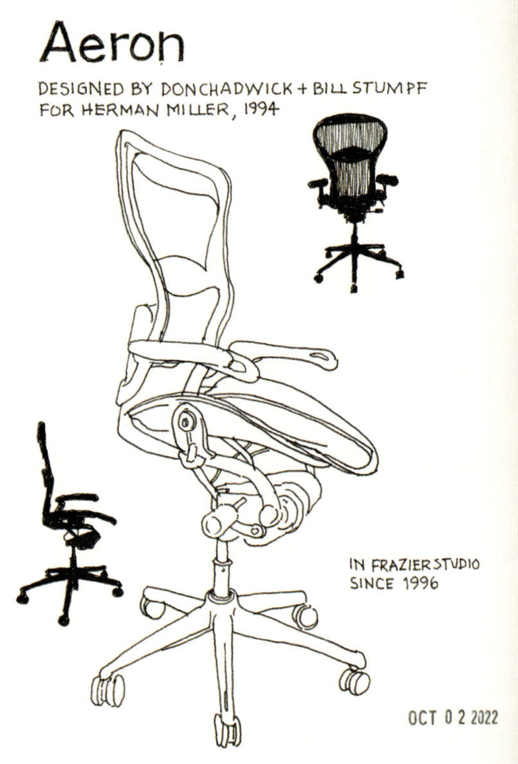

Sketchbooks, 1997–2022

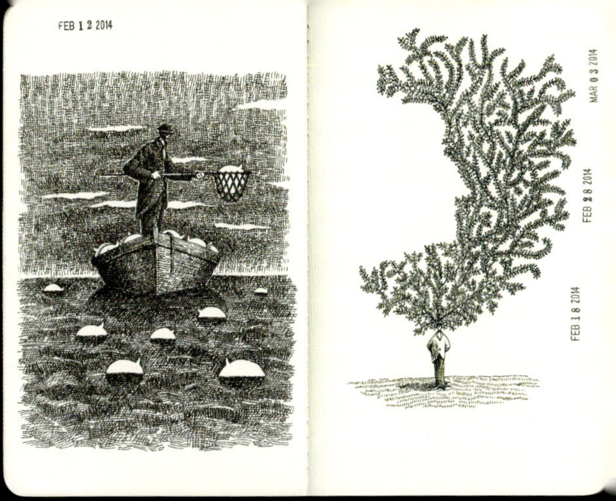

Love notes.

Suz and I met in 1978 as young graphic designers working at the same Palo Alto design studio. We've been married since 1981. She is an artist maintaining two studios—one for oil painting and one for copperplate etching. She goes to one of them every day.

When we travel, we map our trips around the museums and galleries we will visit and the restaurants we'll dine in. We spend the days looking at art and the evenings talking about it.

In 2015, we traveled to London for a week. Our first stop was the Tate Modern, one of our favorite museums. We particularly wanted to see a retrospective of Agnes Martin, one of Suz's favorite artists. I watched her immerse herself in Martin's enormous body of work. All of it is linear and precise, and typically employs the most delicate colors and graphite lines. In front of one particular painting, I watched as Suz leaned her body, tilted her head, and locked her gaze on a single line. It would appear that no one else was in the museum, not even me, just Suz and Agnes, entranced in conversation. A precious moment I captured on my iPhone.

That evening, in our Clerkenwell Airbnb—while having a glass of wine and cheese—I drew that moment in my sketchbook as a small remembrance of how lovely it was to witness.

The next day, we were in the Phillips Collection and it happened again. Suz stood staring at a massive Mark Bradford piece, then leaned into a detail as if to inspect the nylon rope he had sanded to a pulp. I was struck by the graphic shape of her body, all in black, looking as if she was about to give the painting a kiss. She was having that conversation again. Moments later, she stood staring again into a field of Damien Hirst dots, mesmerized. And again, that evening I drew both of those moments in my sketchbook.

Later in that trip came the Nic Fiddian-Green horse's head in *Marble Arch*. Unfamiliar with his work, we both stood speechless in utter awe of its scale, patina, and "on-point" orientation. Suz stood dwarfed beneath it as if she had gone through the incredible shrinking machine.

From those days forward, I would take notice of how Suz was looking at the art we were visiting. What did she see that I didn't? Many times, I would look for her to point me to something I might miss. Other times, I'd back up and take in the dance she would have with a particular piece. Unannounced to her, I would capture these on my iPhone, later to be entered into my sketchbook.

I would continue to journal these art visits, only rarely showing them to Suz or anyone else. Each sketch recorded a trip to another city, country, or just our local San Francisco Museum of Modern Art.

At one time, we attended the opening gala of the SFMoMA in 2016, which was a party unlike any we had ever attended. From the new, unchristened building to the fellow artists to the food to the booze—it was surreal. Perhaps most memorable was the first hour, when we entered the room housing the permanent collection to view several Sol Lewitt walls, without a soul other than the two of us present. You could hear a pin drop and all but touch the walls. This was full immersion. That moment made it into my sketchbook as well.

We would attend a similar event, though not in a new building, at LACMA. As if on cue, Suz stood in near-silhouette under a Henri Matisse ceramic piece, reminding us of how grand—in scale and spirit—his work is.

In 2020, at the start of the pandemic, we paid a visit to Gallery 16 in San Francisco, a staple in the San Francisco art scene and a regular part of our art diet. We went with the intention of seeing the artist David Hytone for the first time and having lunch in the city. An art field trip. We were completely taken by his paintings and one piece in particular, which we bought on the spot. It hangs in our home today. In the sketch (upper right, opposite page), Suz's body language had the "we must have this" lean to it!

Later in 2020, when the quarantine restrictions were loosening, we paid a visit to the de Young to view the work of Bay Area artists who had been accepted into an open call exhibition. Suz was one of those artists and stood beneath her painting, simultaneously in pride and disbelief at the moment and the place. Surprisingly, she looked at the piece as if it were the first time seeing an unknown artist—in conversation once again.

At this point, I've entered over sixty of these "occasional" sketches in my books and I'm reminded that some of the less intentional efforts in our lives are often the most precious. I'd like to think my sketches are as unaware of their surroundings as Suz is when she is looking at art—and they are a slight homage to what she has shown me. As any artist will attest, we draw what we love.

Birds of a feather

Editorial, *Made in America*
Arrive magazine/Amtrac, 2018

MADE IN USA
frazier

Corporate editorial
Trust magazine, Baillie Gifford, 2023

Book cover, *Il Giocatore Invisible (The Invisible Player)*
Oscar Moderni, 2019

Corporate branding/advertising
Navigant Corporation, 2010

Interview by Kirk Citron

Writer, Creative Director, Founder AKQA

Full disclosure: I've known Craig for thirty-five years, and he's one of my closest friends. We've worked together, traveled together, been fired off projects together, and spent many long evenings talking about art, design, writing, music, and creativity. Still, I had a few questions.

When we first met, you were still a designer. But you'd also been doing some ads for Steelcase that I admired. What did you learn from doing advertising?

It changed the way I thought about visuals. I realized they should be complementary to the copy, not just a picture of what the words are already saying. Reading Bernbach completely reorganized the way I approach the page. The whole is greater than the sum of the parts. Another thing I noticed is that advertising has a responsibility to actually make something happen, to provoke some kind of response in the reader. Designers don't usually think that way. So I always try to ask, what are we really trying to do? And that completely changes the way you illustrate.

What is it about drawing that you like?

I like drawing because it's personal. It's a solitary act, but it can protect you from feeling alone, from being isolated, from feeling different. It's a way to feel some sense of yourself when you're completely by yourself. Beyond that, it's a reflection of how you see things. I'm also aware that not everyone can do it, so there's a bit of identity attached to it. Because, you know, I'm not a musician, and I'm not an athlete—it's just what I do. It's a satisfying way to make a living.

What is it that keeps you drawing?

There is no thrill like drawing a picture that you didn't expect to draw. Where you might have kind of imagined it, but it came out even better. It's what every creator feels, that you've produced something out of nothing. It's remarkably satisfying. I think particularly at this stage of the game, it's probably the best use of my skills, the best use of my intellect, it's the best use of all that I feel. It's proof of work. It's proof of work, that you got something done that day.

Advertising
Steelcase, 1990

How do you think your personality is reflected in your work?

I've always been a smart aleck. It's the way I am in conversation. It's the way I am with my best friends. I enjoy that kind of repartee. And so I think there's something askew inside that I'm trying to visualize, a kind of a spark, if you will. A lot of times I'm illustrating things that are very, very serious, and so it's not unlike what I would do in conversation—to somehow lighten the thing up and search for an optimistic side to it. To keep things interesting.

What do you think clients want when they hire you?

I don't actually know what they want. I know what I want them to want: my best work. The really good clients are familiar with me, they want that thing that I do. And I don't know what that is completely, but it's partially an intellectual thing and partially a graphic thing. They want their message packaged the way I do it. And when a project doesn't go well, it's because that's not what they really wanted.

How do you handle rejection?

It never feels good, but it's part of the job. If I miss the mark on the sketches, I'll just start over. But if something happens mid-project, it's usually because somebody got involved at the last minute and changed the assignment. I was once doing ads for Chevrolet when they introduced this big van that had doors on two sides, and the campaign was about work in/fun out (page 130). So I did a sketch with a carpenter loading in wood on one side and a dog jumping out through a hoop held by a clown on the other. It was just a funny way of making the point. But then the CEO saw it and said, "I hate clowns. They scare me." There's no win out of that.

What's the best compliment you ever got?

When my son Drew was about five or six he was looking at one of my little promo books. Page by page, looking really closely. I asked, "Drew, what are you doing?" And he said, "I'm looking for that thing you do, in each drawing." He was already aware of this thing that existed in most of my illustrations— and took pleasure in finding it. That was high praise.

Advertising, *Fun in, Fun out*
Chevrolet, 1999

Corporate editorial
Trust magazine, Baillie Gifford, 2022

Annual report
Whitehead Institute Research, 2014

Editorial, *Retirement Options*
Wall Street Journal, 2014

Book cover, *Women, Language, and Power*
Susannah Baldwin, 2022

Collateral
Bank of America, 2017

Collateral and advertising
University of California, Riverside, 2011

Collateral and advertising
University of California, Riverside, 2010

The Mac.

In 1984, I bought the first Macintosh for my office manager to keep the books. It had 128k of memory. I knew this was the start of something, but had no idea the entire business of graphic design was about to change. Until then, typography was specified and set by typographers and word experts. Photos were shot on film and—heaven forbid—then retouched by experts as necessary. Logos, charts, graphs, and maps were inked by hand with technical pens on vellum. Illustrations were painted and scanned on expensive drum scanners. Art for printing was pasted on boards, frequently with color applied by trained "film strippers" at the printer. Translation: client changes were expensive. The finished printed results reflected the patience and craftsmanship of myriad experts. It was difficult to rush a project. Things were designed to last—they just took a long time to make.

By 1995, typographers' shops were shuttered, printers were consolidating and "desktop publishing" was in full takeover mode. We watched as businesses and professional practices vanished before our eyes. We all felt vulnerable, and worse still, we had little voice in the matter.

About the same time, I was invited to a gathering of creatives in Maine, hosted by Russell Preston Brown, Adobe's lead evangelist for a new product called Photoshop. In a room of colleagues, photographers, illustrators, and designers, all of us were wide-eyed being introduced to this amazing new software. Clearly, it would be a game-changer—for good or bad.

Within two years, I had begun my transition to illustration and was experimenting with Photoshop.

Though it was primarily targeted toward photo manipulation, I discovered that it enabled me to complete analog drawings on the computer—ready to print. Photoshop was my new coloring tool.

Since those early days, I have kept a healthy relationship between my drawing board and the computer. It's easy to jump on the computer under the assumption that we are accelerating the process. Deadlines have a way of corrupting the necessary "think time" in the race to the finish line. I maintain that polish rarely trumps content. I prefer to use the speed of executing a solution as an allowance for more time to uncover new ideas and nurture them.

It's not an either/or matter, it's an equation of proportion. I go heavy on the analog and light on the digital. A rush to digital runs the risk of making "thin" content. Pen on paper keeps the mind fixed on message and intent, and suspends the art of execution. It also trains us to develop the skills to recognize an idea in its infancy without the lure of shine. Sketching is the most efficient stage of prototyping once we learn to recognize a good idea amidst the necessary meanderings that lead us there.

I'm drawn to the blemishes and accidents that come from working with the hand. Most software is designed to do just the opposite, to eliminate imperfection and character. When everyone uses the same tools, we get a homogenized sameness—a dangerous place for career creatives. I think it's important to keep your 'hand' in your work. Ideas have to be drawn out, figuratively and literally. I love my Mac, and use it every day. I just use it for the right things.

Editorial, *Tax Time*
The New York Times, 2018

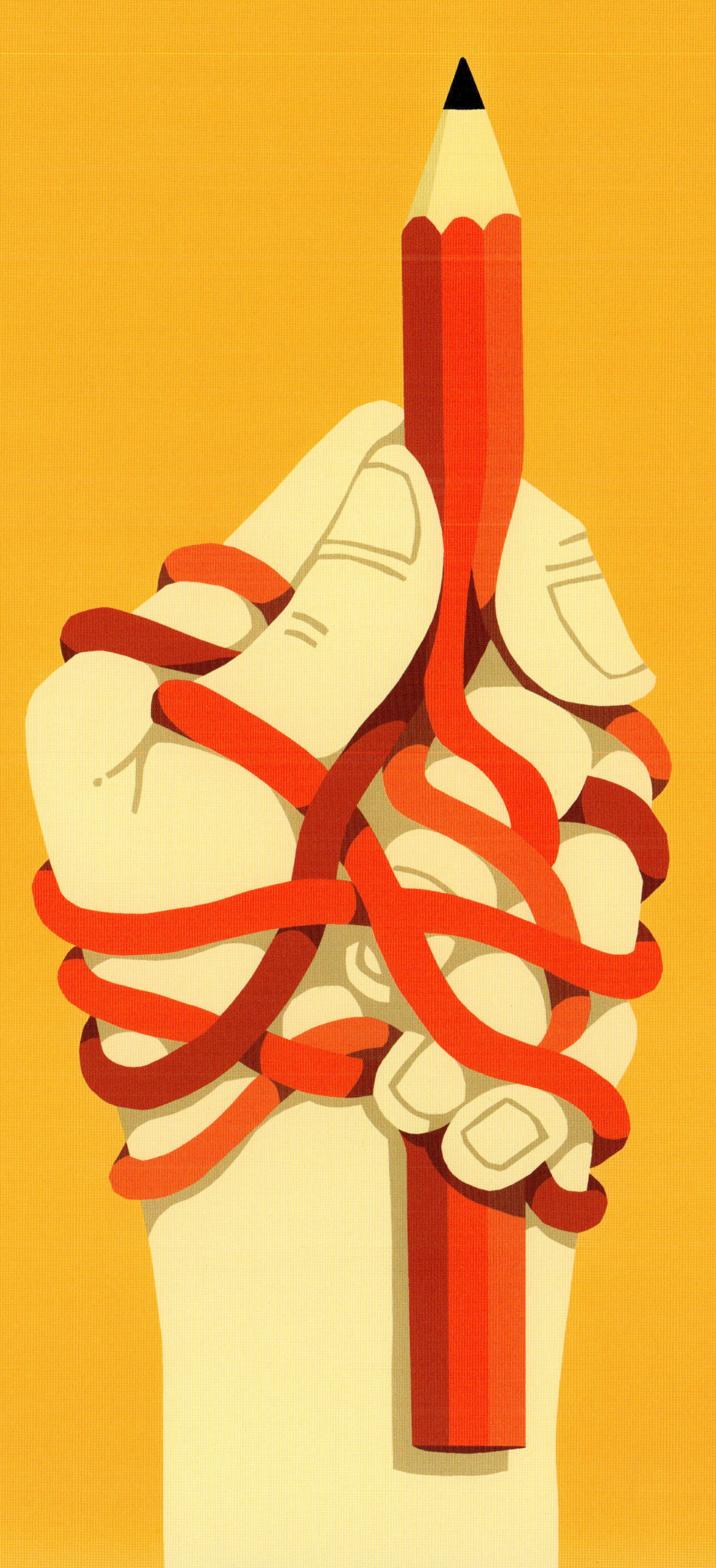

"It is not the critic who counts; not the man who points out how the strong
man stumbles, or where the doer of deeds could have done them better.
The credit belongs to the man who is actually in the arena, whose face is marred by dust
and sweat and blood; who strives valiantly; who errs, and comes short
because there is no effort without error and shortcoming;
actually strive to do the deeds; who knows the great enthusiasms, the great
devotions; who spends himself in a worthy cause; who at the best knows in
the end the triumph of high achievement, and who at the worst, if he fails,
at least fails while daring greatly, so that his place shall never be with those
cold and timid souls who knew neither victory nor defeat."
The Illustrated Voice

iPhone
POSTITS
kingart.
MICRON COLOR
MICRON SEPIA
GRAPHITE + XACTO
PENS
MICRON BLACK

Corporate editorial
Trust magazine, Baillie Gifford, 2021

Restaurant print
Sushi Ran, 2000

Restaurant print
Sushi Ran, 2006

Rocket man.

My dad was a mechanical engineer and a colonel in the Air Force—specifically the Department of Defense. He worked on top-secret projects, so he couldn't talk about his work. (Nuclear secrets don't make for good dinner conversation.) In the military, you get assigned the job and where you will do it according to your skill set, not necessarily your passion or choice. This made it hard to learn much about his work or ambition. I learned other lessons.

My first memory of my dad's mechanical prowess was the engineless go-cart he built for my brothers and me. Unlike my friends' go-carts, steered by pulling on a rope attached to the front axle, our go-cart used wheels from our red wagon and had an actual steering wheel. It employed a "compound lever"—a mechanism made with a hand-sawed steering wheel attached to a shaft made from a broomstick, wrapped with nylon rope that went through a series of pulleys. You steered just as you'd steer a car. It was not only sophisticated, it was the coolest go-cart on the block. I would make that identical cart for my son twenty years later.

The bicycle served as the perfect classroom. Aside from teaching us to ride it, my dad stressed that ownership comes with care and responsibility. I learned that in order to truly understand how something works, you have to take it apart and put it back together. It's a lesson I never forgot. Since we usually bought used bikes, at some point we would paint the frame. Another perfect teachable moment. Dad would insist that the quality of the paint job was a product of the prep. A tough concept to absorb for an eleven-year-old. I would learn the hard way that you can't cover up sins with spray paint. It's about sanding first until the surface is perfectly smooth. You feel the quality of your sanding with the back of your fingers, not the palm of your hand. Painting teaches patience.

My dad made things around the house and at work, and even designed the world's fastest rocket sled (Mach 7) in 1970. Despite my dad's skills, he had little knowledge or interest in design except for European sports cars. He had Austin Healeys, Jaguars, and a Morgan—on which I learned to polish to concours level. He didn't care much about furniture, fashion, or architecture—and certainly not art. He didn't know what graphic design was until I explained what I did for a living. Though design was not much a part of his world, he had a love for solving problems.

He thought about things in mechanical terms. How they worked or why they didn't. To a great extent, he was a visual thinker not unlike Temple Grandin. He never kept a sketchbook. A napkin or an envelope usually sufficed to jot down an idea. At work, he was supported by other engineers and draftsmen who would further explore and bring his sketches into production. In essence, I suppose he was a mechanical creative director. He worked this way in the office and at home. If I struggled to make something, he'd grab an envelope and sketch out his directive. He explained form through function, often drawing the way something was built to demonstrate how to fix it. Unknowingly, I was learning that ideas could be expressed visually with nominal formality. Though he never verbalized it, simplicity was a primal mode for him. He believed nothing was too complicated to be fixed. The ability to break things down to their essence was a core skill he possessed—and passed down. If you can draw out the problem, you can probably solve it.

Editorial illustration
Arrive magazine, Amtrac, 2013

Corporate editorial
Trust magazine, Baillie Gifford, 2020

Personal
Craig Frazier Studio, 2013

Personal
Craig Frazier Studio, 2021

Editorial
Arrive magazine, Amtrac, 2015

I like to bring things to the brink of explanation, then take one step back.

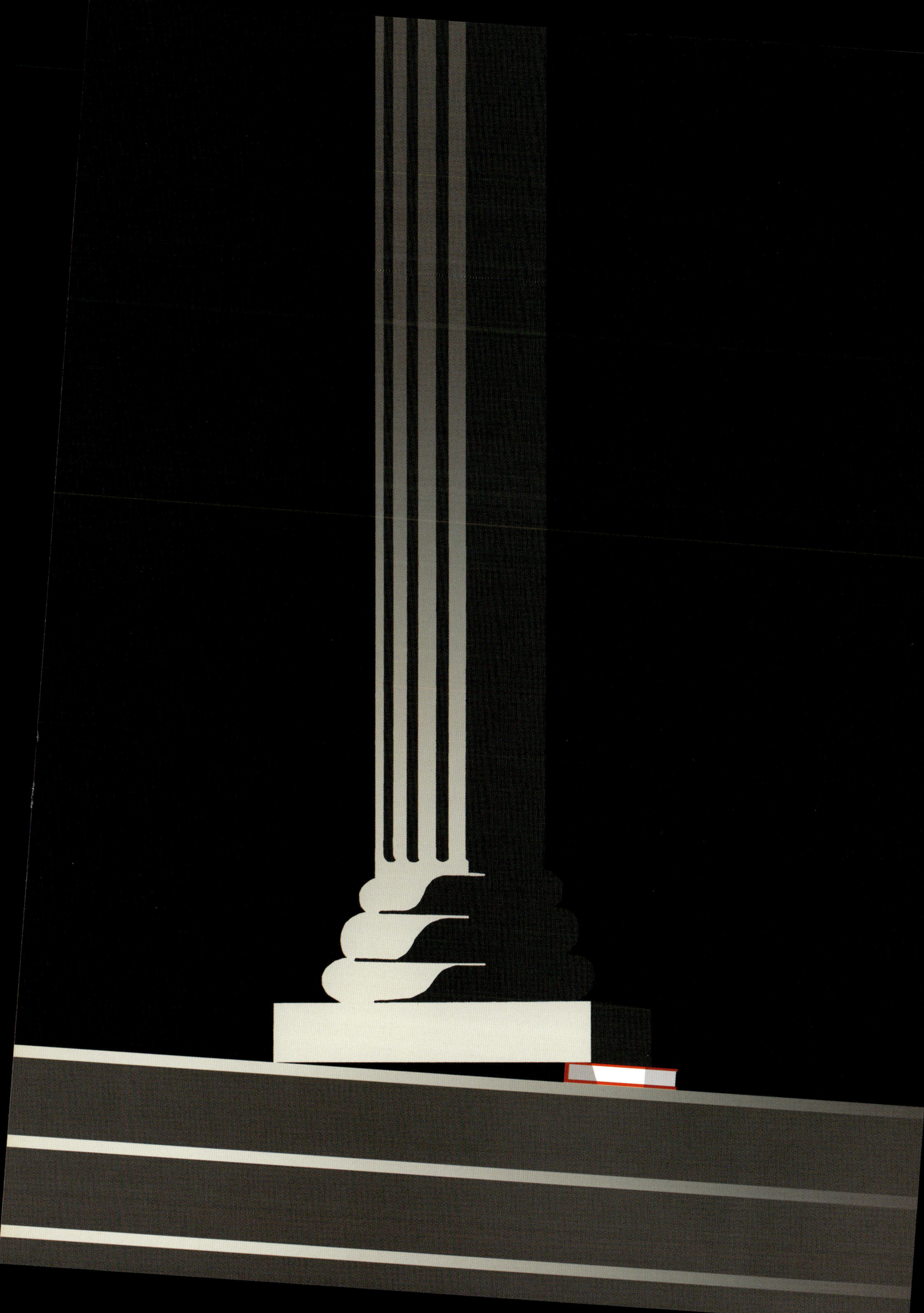

< Editorial, *Student Activism*
Deseret magazine, 2021

Collateral
Realm Cellars, 2022

Collateral
Salesforce, 2006

Corporate editorial, *Faith Over Fear
Trust* magazine, Baillie Gifford, 2023

Posters and postage.

A postage stamp in your hand is the visual equivalent of a poster at thirty feet away. They are design cousins. Both have to communicate quickly from a particular distance. Though you can get closer to a poster, a stamp doesn't reveal much greater information at six inches than it does at twenty-four inches. The purpose is identical for both—convey a clear message at maximum viewing distance. Simplicity in idea and execution rule.

Coincidentally, I work out ideas for both posters and stamps at the same size. I create a sketch about an inch tall, appropriately called a thumbnail. I have literally done this since my introduction to design in college, sketching small, quickly and plentifully. The beauty is that a thumbnail can only contain so much information, in this case, just the right amount for the final product. A common mistake is to find the idea at thumbnail and then overdraw it at a larger scale, adding superfluous detail and information. In a stamp, this results in an image that the viewer can't resolve, because we can only get so close. In a poster, too much detail risks impeding its "street impact" by compromising the instant readability. Too much information sacrifices effectiveness. It's tricky.

Both of these design products call out for maximum simplicity, not only aesthetically but also functionally. It's no surprise that the very best poster designers are often the best trademark designers—experts in simplicity, symbols, and restraint. You can't think about how to design a poster without recalling the work of the greats like Paul Rand, Ivan Chermayeff, Tom Geismar, Herbert Matter, Saul Bass, Ikko Tanaka, Per Arnoldi, and Massimo Vignelli. All have portfolios brimming with both posters and world-class trademarks.

As a medium for messaging, posters and postage stamps differ considerably. Stamps typically speak to universal messages of life, seasons, places, people, and commemorative events. Whereas posters serve to promote and provoke. Theater, concerts, political candidates—and most profoundly, protest—find voice in posters. They speak to their audiences in the public forum. They are the torch bearers of announcement, conversation, and persuasion. The overarching commonality for designers is our participation in the public conversation. Be it main street windows or an envelope, the privilege of putting down our best marks into the world never tires.

Event Poster
Fillmore Jazz Festival, 2015

JULY 4 & 5, 2015
FILLMORE
FESTIVAL
JAZZ

Postage stamp design and illustration
Issued and unpublished designs
US Postal Service, Royal Mail, 2005 - 2023

Declaration of Independence
US Postal Service, 2011

Scouting Commemorative
US Postal Service, 2012

Love
US Postal Service, 2006

Event poster
Fillmore Jazz Festival, 2007

Commemorative poster
Town Cutler, 2011

Event poster
Sushi Ran, 2002

Social poster
Graphis International, 2022

Social poster
Craig Frazier Studio, 2020

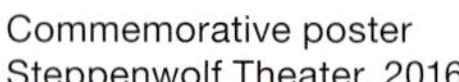

Commemorative poster
Steppenwolf Theater, 2016

Awareness poster
National Campaign Against Youth Violence, 2000

Awareness poster
Craig Frazier Studio, 2001

Awareness poster
Wine Country Rise, 2017

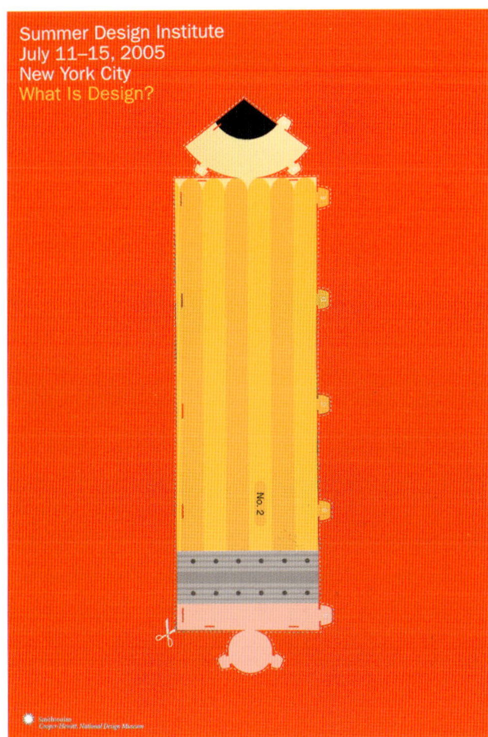

Promotional poster
The Oxbow School, 2003

Event poster
Cooper-Hewitt National Design Museum, 2005

Event poster
Marin Breast Cancer Council, 2003

Promotional poster
DuMOL Winery, 2023

The Graphic Design
Communication
Department at
Philadelphia University
and AIGA/Philadelphia
present a lecture by
Craig Frazier
April 20, 2004
Tuttleman Auditorium
Reception 6:00 pm
Lecture 7:00 pm

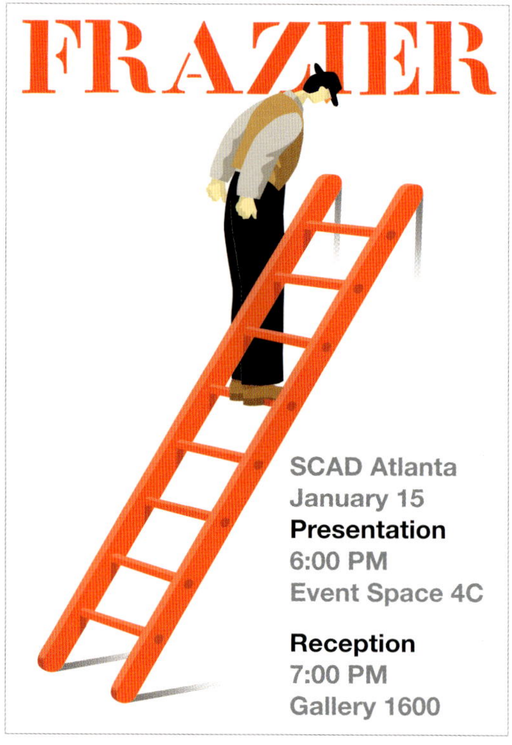
FRAZIER
SCAD Atlanta
January 15
Presentation
6:00 PM
Event Space 4C

Reception
7:00 PM
Gallery 1600

CRAIG FRAZIER
THE COLOR OF
CREATIVITY
Craig Frazier
Pop-up Exhibition
The Gallery at Miami Ad School
July 19–September 13, 2019
Reception July 19, 6:30–8:30 PM
All work is for sale. The
proceeds benefit Miami Ad
School's Minority Scholarship
fund. The scholarships help
minorities start creative careers
at the school's locations in
Atlanta, Miami, New York and
San Francisco.
MIAMI AD SCHOOL
@ PORTFOLIO CENTER

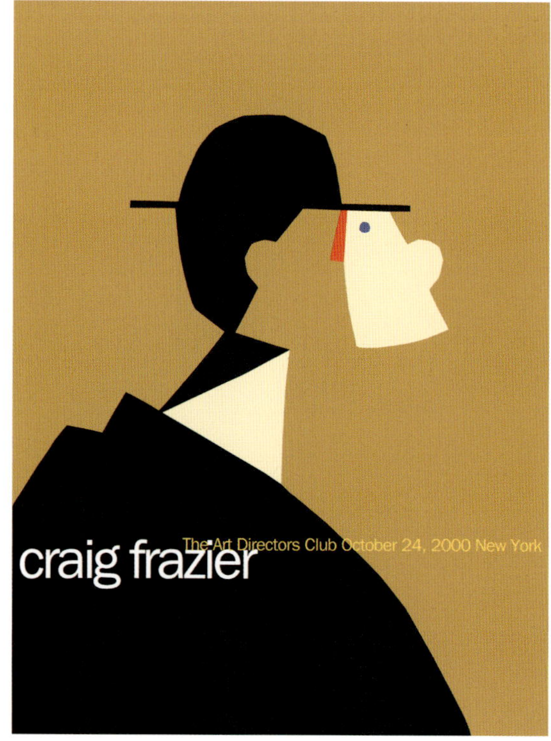
The Art Directors Club October 24, 2000 New York
craig frazier

Craig Frazier
Seeing the Signs
Wednesday, March 6
6:30pm
Room B125
Trafalgar Campus
Honours Bachelor
of Illustration
All Illustration
Students Welcome
Sheridan

Night night.

Tell someone at a party that you've done a few kids' books and they immediately want an introduction to your publisher—they've got a book they've been dying to write. Worse, they ask if you want to illustrate it. How hard can it be? It's just for kids after all.

Kids' books are deceptively difficult to make. A renowned editor I once worked with told me there is no harder audience to write for than kids—it's all about brevity and complimenting the drawings. "The words and pictures can't mirror each other, they have to add up to something greater. Keep it simple—kids know the difference." Agreed. Good advice for all illustration assignments in general.

Publishers always want to know what age you are targeting and the truth is, I never know—and I don't really design from that perspective. I want to make a story that parents want to read to their kids at whatever age they want. I'm secretly trying to delight the adults through their children.

Children's book, *Going*
Harper Collins, 2019

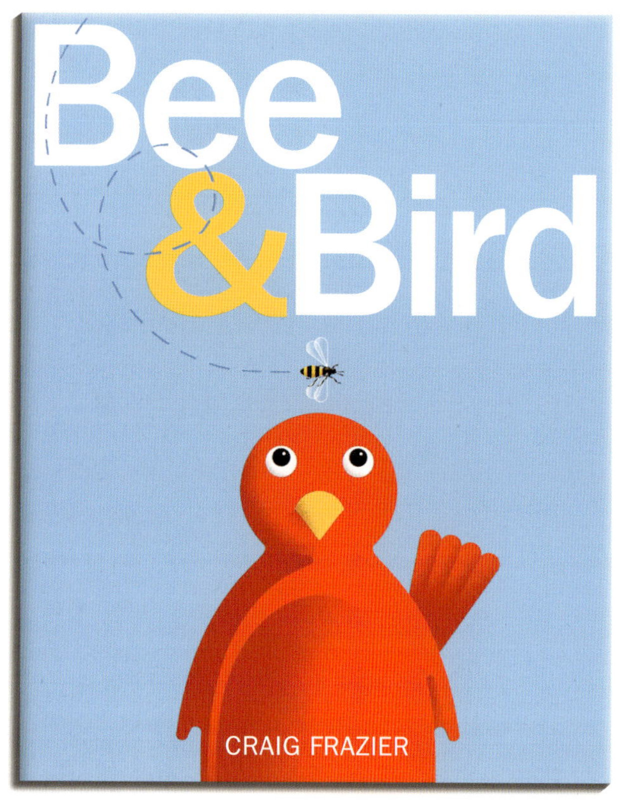

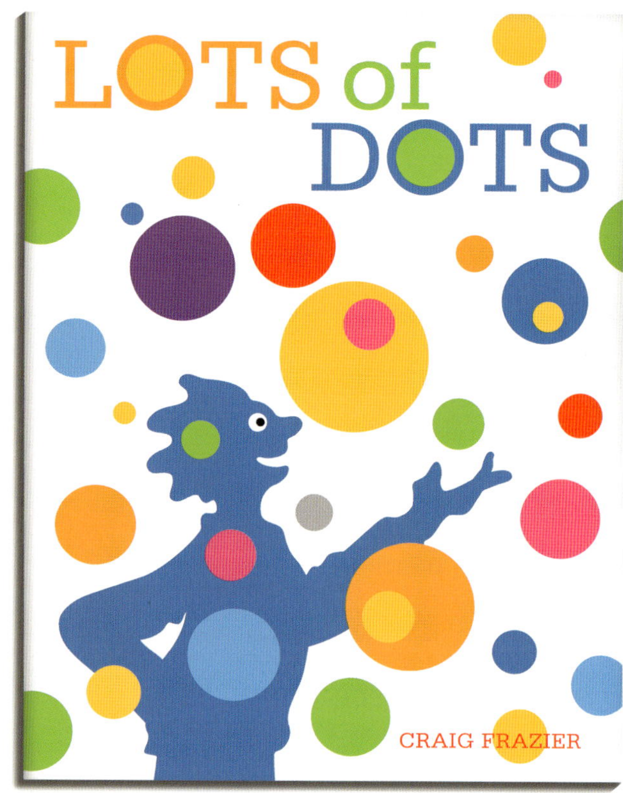

Children's book, *Bee & Bird*
Roaring Brook Press, 2010

Children's book, *Sitting*
Harper Collins, 2014

Children's book, *Lots of Dots*
Chrolicle Books, 2010

Children's book, *Trucks Roll!*
Simon & Schuster, 2007

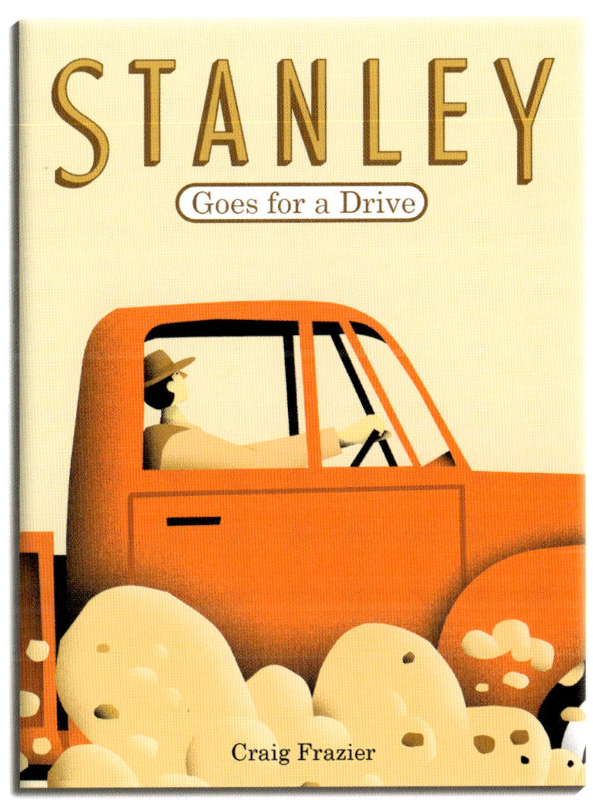

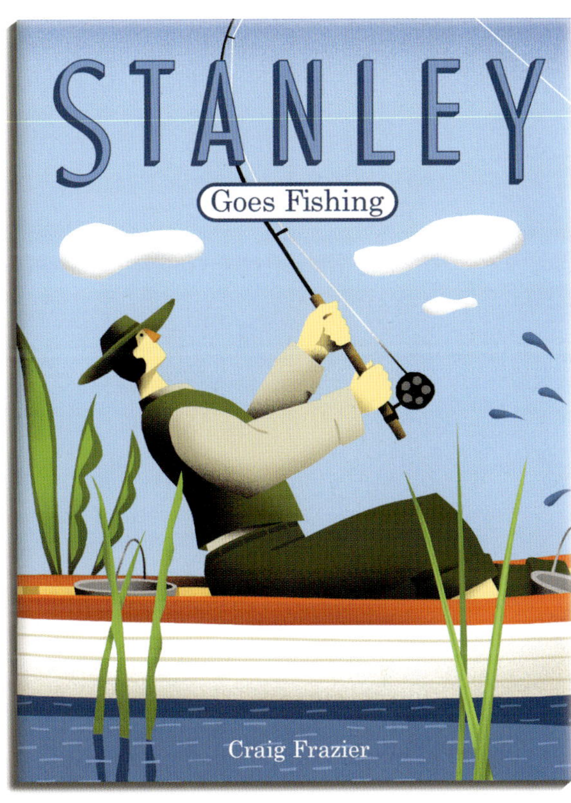

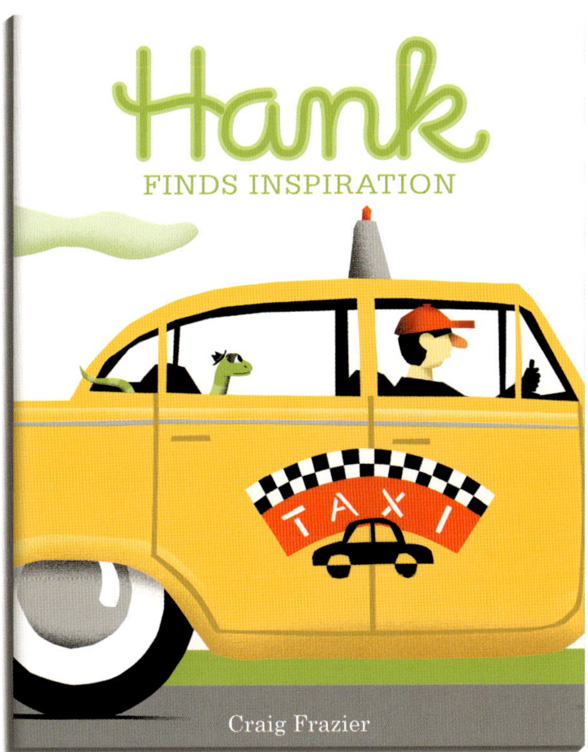

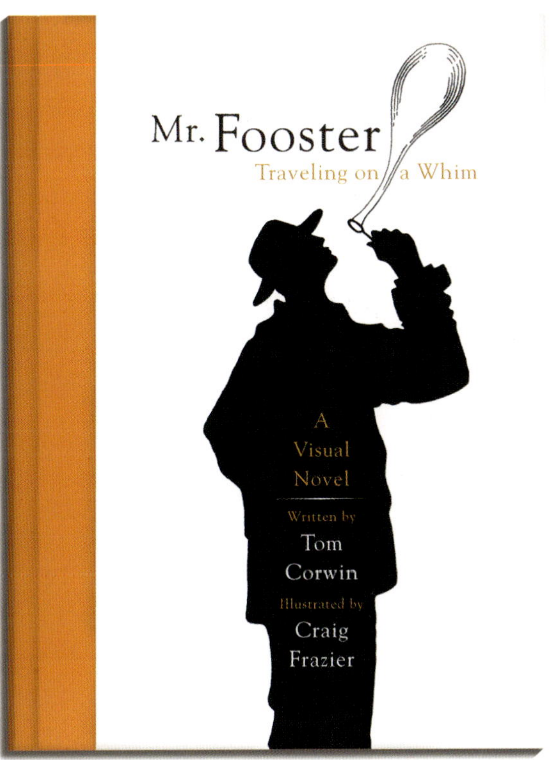

Children's book, *Stanley Goes for a Drive*
Chronicle Books, 2004

Children's book, *Hank Finds Inspiration*
Roaring Brook Press, 2008

Children's book, *Stanley Goes Fishing*
Chronicle Books, 2006

Children's/adult book, *Mr. Fooster Traveling on a Whim*
Doubleday, 2008

Children's book, *Stanley Goes Fishing*
Chronicle Books, 2006

Children's book, *Stanley Mows the Lawn*
Chronicle Books, 2005

Children's book, *Trucks Roll!*
Simon & Schuster, 2007

Children's book, *Hank Finds Inspiration*
Roaring Brook Press, 2008

Children's/adult book, *Mr. Fooster Traveling on a Whim*
Doubleday, 2008

I feel particularly lucky to work in
a field that, on a good day, asks and
rewards your visual opinion.

Personal
Craig Frazier Studio, 2006

Corporate editorial
Trust magazine, Baillie Gifford, 2019

Conference identity
Sonoma Valley Author's Festival, 2016

Wine label
Realm Cellars, 2014

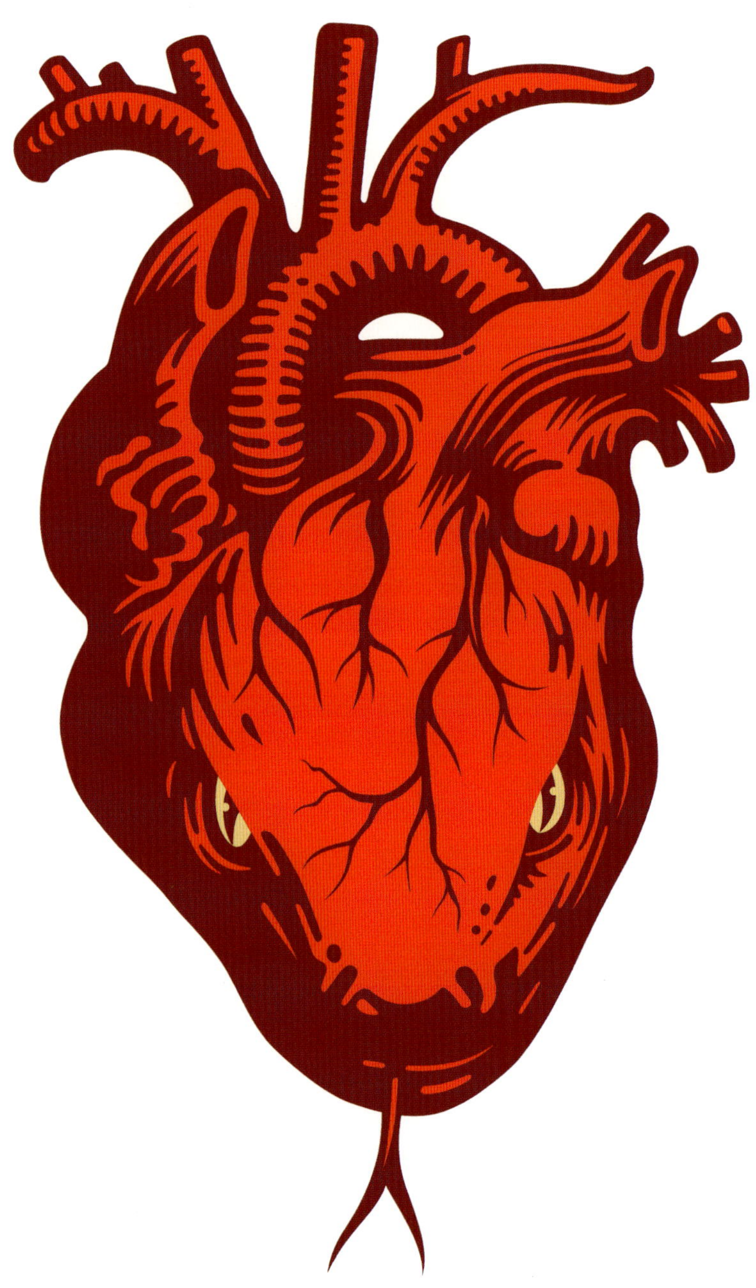

Advertising, *Deadly Heart Danger*
Pfizer, 2018

Editorial, *GOP Civil War*
Deseret Magazine, 2021

Editorial
Deseret Magazine, 2022

Editorial, Op/ed
The New York Times, 2005

Editorial, *Can't Get Away*
Arrive magazine/Amtrac, 2016

frazier

Editorial, *Smart Eating*
Time Magazine, 2006

Merchandise
John Fairey Garden, 2023

Acknowledgments

After graduating college in 1978, I landed in Palo Alto, California, at a brand-new design firm. They hired me because I could draw. The job itself was life-changing—even more so was the designer hired before me, who would mentor my infant skills. We would marry some three years later.

Suz Frazier. You have been with me this entire wild ride—every minute. In fact, you have been air traffic control. Your unshakable belief in me has enabled a near lifelong experiment. You have never had any doubt—at least that I witnessed. That is love, and there is no earthly power greater. Thank you dear.

Daniele and Drew Frazier. You show me that when we put ourselves into what we make, we find meaning. You changed my career to the best job on earth (page 34). You have reminded to be playful, simple, and—above all—human. May you each see a little of yourselves in these pages.

Thank you Drew for finding the "thing" in my work from a tiny age and teaching me that if you want an honest opinion, ask a child.

Thank you Daniele for offering up your unequivocal wisdom and saying, "you gotta do this book, Dad."

I want to thank my comrades for your kind remarks (page 100). I hold your opinions—and work—in the highest esteem. *Steve Heller, Ivan Chermayeff, Joe Morse, Christoph Neimann, Kit Hinrichs, Michael Schwab, Ken Segall, Karin Hibma Cronan, Kirk Citron, Richard Danne, Paul Rogers, Emiliano Ponzi, and Antonio Castro.*

Ken Segall. I am honored to have had your eyes, words, and knowledge of the subject in service of my story. Not only did I learn a lot, you have made me make better sense. Simply, thank you Ken.

Michael Rylander. You are the true ambassador of simplicity. Thank you for your comradeship and critical comment on this book. And thank you for introducing me to Ken Segall.

Kirk Citron. Thank you for your smart words in this book and your love of a good idea, and more so, your friendship.

Hank Richardson. You have put me in front of decades of wide-eyed students asking me "why," and taught me to make the answer personal. Your heartfelt words in the opening pages touch me deeply. Thank you Hank.

Smeeta Mahanti. Thank you for your keen eye that captured me and my studio in such honest light.

Susannah Baldwin. The questions you asked led me to present a far deeper, more personal story in these pages. Thank you for reminding me why we are here.

Lance Hidy. You championed me in your tenure at *Harvard Business Review.* You showed me good writing and asked me to explain it in pictures. Thank you Lance.

Gregg Berryman. Thank you for my college design education and teaching me to make thumbnails.

Andy Bosman. You put my work to the highest task of corporate branding for years without condition. Thank you Andy.

Charlotte Sheedy. You shepherded me into the world of children's books with great laughter and affection. Thank you Charlotte.

Michael Schwab. You showed me that the life of a California illustrator is both desirable and within reach. Thanks pal.

Simone Silverstein. You inspired me to keep my writing real if I wanted it read. Thank you Simone.

Kelly Griego. Thank you for guiding the content of my introduction. Your counsel set the course.

Joni Pon. You managed my design business and my illustration practice until 2018. You maintained studio order, welcomed every single client, and watched every drawing go out the door. Thank you Joni.

Hall Kelley. As the story goes, you hired me for my first design job much because I could draw. We'll go with that. Thank you Hall.

Conrad Jorgensen. Thank you for trusting me to be your partner when we were just kids. We learned that half the game is the courage to get in it.

Mr. Cash. You were my seventh grade English teacher that taught me that you can draw a sentence if it is properly written. Thank you.

Jan Collier. You represented me in the early days and instantaneously put me in the game. Thank you Jan.

Griff Williams. You have brought my work to the walls of myriad clients and offered the encouragement to make this book—and especially present the Amberliths! Thank you.

Gordon Goff. Thank you for your instant belief in this book and ensuring that it sees an audience. Thank your team at Oro Editions for their expertise in making it happen.

Chip Smith. Thank you for providing the biggest magnetic wall in California for serious debate amongst us critics.

Jeff Hurn. Thank you for making the "Book Meets Barn" video, it may be the book's finest moment.

I want to thank the hundreds of clients who have had faith in me and my ideas, and were particularly willing to say a lot with a little, along with a pinch of humor.

The steel critique barn, Petaluma, California
250 feet of book and 600 magnets, June 2023